PRAISE FOR *I*

MW01592394

"This book is a revelation. A 'must read' for sales people. Willy Loman would not have met the fate that he did had he been exposed to its contents. And it is written in the brisk writing style of a western novel."

—Alan Cimburg, CPAE
National Speakers Association past director

"*Hired Gun* is THE book every sales manager and business CEO has looked for, longed for, and never found! If you hire salespeople, buy a copy for every one of them."

—Dottie Walters, CSP
author of *Never Underestimate the Selling Power of a Woman*
(Wilshire Book Co.); and *Speak and Grow Rich*
with Lilly Walters (Prentice Hall-Simon Schuster)

"*Hired Gun* is a must read for every person in sales. If you want to get to the top and stay there, or you're already at the top and want to stay there, read this book. Robert Workman's reality focus is a must for all of us."

—Thomas J. Winninger, CSP, CPAE
1995 Cavett winner and NSA past president

"This is a great, hard hitting book, full of punchy examples and anecdotes that tell it like it *really* is in the fast moving world of sales and sales management."

—Brian Tracy, CPAE
President, Brian Tracy Learning Systems

"If you're considering a career in sales, or if you're already in sales and need some fresh inspiration, read this book. *Laws of the Hired Gun* will give you a unique personal perspective of someone who's 'been there.' Workman's insights are sometimes brazen, sometimes funny, but always interesting! There are some good lessons here."

—Dr. Tony Allesandra, Ph.D., CPAE, CSP
author of *The Platinum Rule* (Warner Books); *Collaborative Selling* (Wiley);
and *Communicating at Work* (Fireside/Simon & Schuster)

"*Hired Gun* is refreshing. It takes no-nonsense success principles and puts them in your face in a fun and fascinating way. This is a book that causes you to tell yourself the truth, while learning truly powerful ways to achieve and keep more success."

—Jim Cathcart, CSP, CPAE
president of National Speakers Association 1988–1989,
winner of the 1993 Cavett Award,
author of *Relationship Selling* (Putnam Publishing Group),
now translated into Chinese, Japanese and Finnish

"A great book for anyone seeking personal excellence and professional success—in sales and in life."

—Nido Qubein, CSP, CPAE
author, *How To Be A
Great Communicator*
1985 Cavett winner and NSA past president
Author: *How to Be a Great Communicator* (John Wiley & Sons, Inc.)

HIRED GUN

**YOU'RE #1,
AND SOMEBODY
HATES IT**

Robert Workman

**Direct Media Marketing, Inc.
Dallas, Texas**

Copyright © 1999 by Robert Workman / All rights reserved.
The phrase "Hired Gun" is a registered trademark. No part of this book may be reproduced in any form without permission in writing from the publisher, except by a reviewer who wishes to quote brief passages in connection with a review written for inclusion in a magazine, newspaper, or broadcast.

Direct Media Marketing, Inc.
2720 Sylvan Ave. Suite 200
Dallas, TX 75212
Phone: 214-749-1150
Toll free: 877-544-1155

Hired Gun website: www.hired-gun.com

Book Production: Phelps & Associates

PRINTED IN THE UNITED STATES OF AMERICA

Publisher's Cataloging-in-Publication
(Provided by Quality Books, Inc.)

Workman, Robert.
    Hired gun : you're #1 and somebody hates it /
Robert Workman. -- 1st ed.
    p. cm.
    Includes bibliographical references.
    LCCN: 98-074583
    ISBN: 0-9666668-5-X (hardcover)
    ISBN: 0-9666668-7-9 (pbk.)

    1. Selling. 2. Sales personnel--Vocational
guidance. 3. Corporate culture--United States.
I. Title

HF5438.25.W67 1999   658.8'5
                         QBI98-1597

TABLE OF CONTENTS

It is not the critic who counts,

not the man who points out how the strong man fails,

or where the doer of good deeds could have done them better.

The credit belongs to the man who is actually in the arena,

whose face is marred by dust and sweat and blood;

who errs, and comes short again and again,

because there is no effort without error and shortcoming.

But who does actually strive to do the deeds,

who knows the great enthusiasms, the great devotions,

who spends himself in a worthy cause;

who at best knows in the end the triumph of high achievement,

and who at the worst if he fails,

at least fails while daring greatly,

so that his place shall never be with those cold and timid souls

who know neither victory or defeat.

— *Theodore Roosevelt, 1910*

FAST FOREWORD

Bob Workman and I have dedicated our lives to studying excellence. I studied Bob as he studied the masters and became a master himself.

With so much written about How To's it seems that what has become lost is what happens to the ones who do truly become successful. Why is it lonely at the top?

Bob has dedicated his life with a passionate obsession to studying the fine line between winners and losers. When I met Bob he was twenty-five, a track and field champion with Bachelor's and Master's Degrees with honors, and was driving a school bus. During the next fast-paced years I watched him grow to achieve an income and lifestyle enjoyed by only the top 2%. The final step of his commitment to self-actualization was to put it on paper, and this book is the result.

—Joseph J. Charbonneau, CSP, CPAE
President, Presentations Inc.
Trophy Club, Texas

PREFACE

Getting to the top isn't the problem, staying there is. The destiny of salespeople of fortune is to emotionally experience mountaintop sunrises and sea trench midnights. First, it is vital that a top producer accepts these ups and downs as occupational hazards; it is then important to know how to deal with them in order to control lightheadedness at the heights and nitrogen narcosis in the depths. *Remaining* #1 requires an entirely different skill set than *becoming* #1. These ultimate lessons in successful selling are what I share with you in *Hired Gun*.

"Gender-Specific Expression"

I practiced diplomatic use of gender in this discourse until the computer's grammar-check function protested my last name as a "gender-specific expression." Get over it. Reform is one thing; the Spanish Inquisition is another. Our social culture is becoming concerned to a fanatical degree with politically correct posturing. If the pundits of this nineties phenomenon have their way, Texas chili will taste like vegetable stew; we'll all live in the 'Burbs, have 2.6 children and drive minivans.

Viva Ferraris—Hooray for martinis—Light up a Churchill cigar! When I talk about a salesman I'm referencing a guy I knew in a particular situation; when I talk about the superlative women I've known in sales, (and according to *Dartnell's 29th Sales Force CompensationSurvey 1996–1997* there are more women in sales today than ever before at 24.1%) I refer to them as saleswomen. Mostly I talk about sales reps, and when I sign my name I make no apologies to any techno-grammarian.

—Robert Workman

THE GUNFIGHTER SYNDROME

Congratulations—you are now or soon will be the #1 sales rep in your organization. That's evident by your action picking up a book like this one. Top producing reps are always on the lookout for something that gives them a competitive edge over their rivals. It's one way they stay at the top.

How we reach the pinnacle of this profession is often a mystery. For example, most successful salespeople have college degrees (65% according to *Dartnell's 29th Sales Force Compensation Survey 1996–1997*)—but not in sales. We don't have many formal settings in which we can learn and practice before entering the real world like traditional schools of law, medicine, architecture or engineering. We do most of our training through extra curricular seminars, books and tapes after we already have a job in sales. It seems many of the companies advertising for someone to create their cash flow want "3 to 5 years selling experience" but don't provide the means to get it.

You accepted the challenge of sales, one that frightens off most who consider it, and for that you have my respect. You took the job, went through training (if any was offered), made joint calls with other reps and your sales manager, read the books, went to seminars, invested money in yourself and the tools of the trade. You worked on weekends while your friends played, and you stayed up late many nights, unable to sleep because your adrenaline was pumping as you mentally prepared for your big presentation the next day, and the next, and the next . . .

It doesn't seem as though you started very long ago, but now you're reaping the rewards of a higher income than your parents ever made, you drive a fine car and make enough money to go places and do things you always wanted. You're on top of the world with a future as bright as a supernova.

So what's that nagging sensation in the back of your mind? Why do you feel those pangs of paranoia when you talk with your colleagues at work about the future? Why do you worry about what the guys upstairs are planning that will affect your job and income? Why is it so difficult to avoid the quilting circle gossip about what's going to happen to the sales team next?

It's called anxiety. Because you're one of the best there is in your profession, you prefer to believe you have more control over what happens to you—but you know you don't. It would only take one stupid decision by some so-called executive who couldn't sell a machine gun to General Custer and you could be out on the street looking for another job. And sales jobs that pay a solid six figures can take time to find, or develop.

Not The Same Old Enchilada

This is not a book about how to sell. You won't find Seven Cutesy Closing Techniques (like the rolling pencil close, please!) or Beowulf-style war stories about How I Made The Greatest Sale In The History Of All Time. I'm full of them (as well as *it*) believe me, but so are you. Shelves in bookstores and racks at car washes already sag from the weight of hundreds of books that preach the gospel of successful selling and other business practices. I've listed my favorites in the back to benefit both salespeople and managers.

Hired Gun helps you understand your unique psychology as a consistent top-producing sales rep, because who you are is a hundred times more important than what you do. And what you do is many times more valuable than most of the jobs in your company.

It examines why you do the things you do, explains why your destiny is to experience extreme feelings of triumph and defeat with an intensity and frequency unknown by any other profession. Most importantly, *Hired Gun* shows you how to deal with the fact that even if you are (and often because you are) the top sales rep in your company, you'll be out on the street before you know it. The bottom line is, you need to be prepared to find another job within the next year. You think this sounds scary? It's not nearly as scary as having it happen to you and not being prepared.

When you're the fastest gun, somebody else is always gunning for you. The problem is, they only come after you on their very best day. It doesn't matter if this also happens to be your worst day; you still have to win. Consequently, you have to be at your best every day, every month.

Top athletes live with this gunfighter syndrome throughout their careers. Imagine the lifetime of pride some duffer has if, on the finest day of golf in his life, he manages to clip Tiger Woods by one stroke, even though The Tiger is ill, having an uncharacteristically lousy day. It's the same in any sport: in college football Notre Dame, Texas, Nebraska, Ohio State, Michigan, USC, Penn State—each one must play its best game every Saturday, because the biggest game of the year for any team that plays them is That Game. Any football team in the NFL can gloat for an entire season if it knocks off the Dallas Cowboys.

In *COWBOYS Have Always Been My Heroes*, Peter Golenbock quotes Drew Pearson, the famous receiver of the Hail Mary pass:

> Everybody had it in for us. And the reason they did was because of our arrogance. Not so much for the Cowboy players on the field. We respected our opponent to the utmost, but it was what Tex Schramm was projecting for the Cowboys as a team. They saw Coach Landry nicely dressed, wearing a tie, a hat on the sideline, and their coaches are in a coaching shirt, a little ugly green jacket. It was what we projected. We projected class. When we traveled, we wore ties. You don't think people recognized that? Sure they did. And if they recognized it, they were going to write about it, and they were going to tell about it. 'This team is class. They do it this way, do it that way,' and a lot of people got tired of hearing that crap. They just

got tired of hearing it. And our opponents used that to help psych themselves up, help motivate themselves to want to beat us. And that's why every time we played anybody, I don't care who it was, the worst team or the best team, they played us like it was their Super Bowl.

In boxing, think about Joe Louis, one of the greatest heavyweight fighters of all time, but after his prime he lost to Rocky Marciano. Allow me to paraphrase a scene from *Coming To America*:

> "Rocky Marciano! Rocky Marciano!
> Every time I mention Joe Louis
> somebody has to bring up Rocky Marciano!"
> "Yeah, but he whooped Joe Louis' ass . . ."
> "Yeah, but Joe Louis was seventy-six years old . . .
> Joe Louis came out of retirement to fight him!"

For this reason, *Hired Gun* teaches you a skill in which top producers don't typically excel: the survival tactic of watching your sides and your back, and knowing when to get out a winner. The reason high achievers are weak in this area is we move through life like a LeMans racer tearing along at 220 mph through Mulsanne. Just as the driver must think of the road eight miles ahead, we live eight days to eight weeks in the future with deals yet to close.

It's a law that as speed increases, peripheral vision narrows. The problem is that our focus is so tight on Doing The Deal that we sacrifice a great deal of proximity awareness. We concentrate so much on the battle at hand that we don't dwell much on political actions subtly taking shape around us.

Your nemeses are not the challenges of selling or managing your finances. You wouldn't be where you are today if they were. Your natural enemies are those very souls who depend on you to be the hunter-gatherer who creates the revenue they need in order to subsist. These are the CFO, COO, GM, VP of Production or other executives or employees not living

H I R E D   G U N   •5•

or dying daily by bringing in revenue to feed the corporate beast. (Sometimes it's even the VP of Sales . . .)

Notice I didn't include the CEO or the entrepreneur who founded the enterprise (often the same person). Of all the people in the organization, this one normally has the keenest appreciation for a top producing sales rep. Entrepreneurs and CEOs know their businesses depend on sales and sales reps. That's why they are The Bosses.

THE GOOD, THE BAD & THE BOURGEOIS

It matters not how strait the gate,
How charged with punishments the scroll,
I am the captain of my fate,
I am the master of my soul.
—William Ernest Henley

he Good News Is: Your security lies not in your job, not in your company, but in yourself. This is true in sales more than any other profession. When you have paid the dues required to become a top sales rep, you can go anywhere, anytime, and make money. If you're truly an all-star, you'll be sought after before you make any decision to change jobs. Imagine Troy Aikman coming up for grabs in the NFL. Why do you think Jerry Jones signed a $50,000,000 contract with this three-time Super Bowl champion and Super Bowl MVP? Troy fills the stadiums. He brings in the cash.

Hired Gun is for and about those who enjoy the freedom they've earned through consistent performance over extended periods of time. It's for the top guns many sales managers wish they had producing their overrides, but also wish they didn't have to manage.

You know who you are: your chief concern is doing the deal, not worrying about whether someone else feels uncomfortable around you merely because you feel good about yourself. You work six days a week to do the best job you possibly can and give 100% of what you have into everything you do. Your motto is,

"WHATEVER IT TAKES TO GET THE JOB DONE."

You are there to produce revenue. You're not there to draw base pay or meet a need for affiliation with colleagues. Social/affiliation needs rank near the bottom of your list at the job, because you're not being paid to make friends, but to do business. If you wanted to make friends you'd join the "Y."

The Bad News Is:

We're not Troy Aikman. Accept the fact that if you're successful in sales, before you know it you'll be selling something different than you're selling now, quite possibly for somebody other than who you're working for now. The irony is, the better you are, the shorter your lifespan will be in your job. The stupidity is, it probably won't be your choice.

Recently, after dinner at Galatoire's in New Orleans, I felt compelled to buy a T-shirt out of a store window on Rue Royale. The slogan on its chest exclaimed: "New Orleans; It's not the heat, it's the stupidity!" Apparently these co-existing factors are not limited to the Crescent City. As a mercenary of sales, heat is an occupational hazard. Unfortunately, so is stupidity. The question is, is it stupidity on the part of the manager who lets the company's top producer hit the door—or on your part for staying too long? That's the dilemma of the Hired Gun.

I know you don't want to believe this, don't want it to be true. You think it won't happen to you; you're good, you're professional, you're loyal. You believe in your company and your job. You work hard; you earn every cent you're paid. Right . . .

Accept it, deal with it, control it and you will be respected, headhunted and successful the rest of your life. But put your blinders on, ignore it, and you're a target for disappointment and confusion when someone allegedly on your own side topples you.

You built your successful position, worked long hours and days to create it. It pays you well. You're not prepared to deal with feelings other than those of being successful. When you're suddenly betrayed you feel strange pangs of despair.

Abnormal feelings in an abnormal situation are normal.

—Law of The Hired Gun

Naturally there are some whiners out there who'll take exception to this reality. They like to impress themselves by hearing their own voices say this theme is negative thinking. Sorry, Harvey; I'm not impressed. This isn't a book of Happy Talk; it's the real deal. This is about making the best hand out of the cards that are dealt to you, good *and* bad. But it goes beyond making lemonade out of lemons—it gets you to prepare for inevitable change and take control of your life. Now that's positive.

Aces and Eights

It isn't that everybody in the company is out to get you; it's that one or two are. And let me tell you, they resent you, hate you, despise you. And they envy you. Why? Because they wish they were you and know that they can't be you, so the only way they can bring themselves up is by dragging you down, even if it means getting you with a bullet in the back. **One of the goals of this book is to have you leaving the table for another game when aces and eights come into your hand.**

Let's identify the probable sources of this paradox:

1) **Your Company:**
    a) It gets sold—so you're out and the acquisition team is in.
    b) For economic reasons, management changes sales policies. The new ones devalue you, your position, your income.
2) **An Executive:** This person is threatened by the glow of your excellence. For reasons of ego and envy, this company official has it out to do you in.
3) **Another Sales Rep:** This one can't beat you on the playing field, so they try to take you out of the game with potshots from the sidelines.

4) **You:** You shoot yourself in the foot due to an insecure self-image that can't cope with the stresses of the lofty position at the top of the heap. Stresses such as:

5) **Your Friends:** The same old gang doesn't hang out with you anymore because you work too hard, make too much money. You look too good, and when you look good they look bad.

Résumés and W-2s

Keep your résumé updated every sixty days. Two months is a long time in many sales environments; a lot can happen. Companies get sold, executives fired, staffs downsized, divisions closed and others opened. In today's business flux it's vital that you're prepared to market yourself at any moment.

There are a lot of handy books and software programs available on effective résumé-writing. The best time to get one and start working is now, while you're doing well. Consider your contribution to the company, major sales you've made, clients with big name recognition you've sold, awards you've received, your W-2.

W-2? That's right. Separate yourself from the phonies. When I interview sales reps, they all claim to have successful track records and to have earned high incomes in previous jobs. So do I. But I back it up with year-end paychecks and copies of W-2s. There it is in black and white; results, no lies or innuendo. I've been told that this can come on a bit strong. Fine; if they don't want strong sales talent they need to look somewhere else, and so do I.

This book isn't for the faint of heart. It's for top carnivores, those who have killer instincts, top producing sales reps. At the risk of preaching to the choir with veterans of corporate wars, it prepares rising hot shots for adverse conditions that lie ahead. I don't mean sales reps who make enough to pay their bills but run out of money before they run out of month. I'm talking about the sales reps others envy, the ones who sell the most deals, bring in the highest revenues, have the highest finish over quota every month, month in and month out.

> **quo.ta** (kwō' tə...) n. 1. a management tool used to measure mediocrity.

Winners and Losers

Let's look at a winner, a Hired Gun in the truest sense of expression—Mickey Spillane. When he wrote *I, The Jury* it sold over six million copies the first year. His next five books averaged some three million copies each, unheard of numbers at the time. In the 1956 book, *Sixty Years of Best Sellers*, Alice Payne Stewart documented that of the ten best-selling American fiction titles ever published, seven were by Mickey Spillane. (He had only written seven books.)

For Mickey, just like for many consistent winners, success did not bring ready acceptance by his peers. In fact, the critics sniped at him with every opportunity. But Mickey Spillane has a secure self-image and knows how to deal with being a winner. In his historical review, *The Fifties*, David Halberstam relates what Spillane endured and how he handled it:

> Certainly, the critics hated him. James Spandoe of the *Herald Tribune* called him "an inept vulgarian." Malcolm Cowley in the *New Republic* called him a dangerous paranoid, sadist, and masochist. Even his own editors seemed a little uneasy with him. Victor Weybright liked to tell reporters that too much was made of the Spillane phenomenon. Such critical salvos did not burden Spillane, who liked to say that he did not care about the critics and that the only critics who mattered were his readers. He

thought the literary world was made up of second-rate writers who wrote about other second-rate writers. It was a world of the Losers. "The Losers?" Terry Southern asked him. "The guys who didn't make it," he answered, "the guys nobody ever heard of." Why, asked Southern, would others want to write about Losers? "Because they can be condescending about the Losers. You know, they can afford to say something *nice* about them. You see, these articles are usually written by Losers—frustrated writers. And these writers resent success. So naturally they never have anything good to say about the Winners." "Is it hard to be a Winner?" Southern asked. "No, anybody can be a Winner—all you have to do is make sure you're not a Loser," he answered.

The Bourgeois:

---

bour·geois (boor' zhwä', boor zhwä') n., pl. bourgeois
1. A person whose attitudes and behavior are marked by conformity to the standards and conventions of the middle class.

Have you ever noticed how many books are written to help middle managers improve? Thousands. Why so many? They need them. Middle managers are by definition bourgeois. They are—in the middle. They don't create; creation comes from the entrepreneur who starts the company, then by the CEO who leads it. Managers don't execute; this is done by those who report to them, those who produce. Managers just manage.

Before you get the impression that I'm unfair to managers, consider your impression of someone who tells you, "I manage," as opposed to a person who says, "I excel; I do whatever it takes to get the job done." Hired Guns have no interest in being Managers. They are interested only in excellence; they are Excellers.

This is not discounting; it's differentiation. Sales reps are one kind of creature; managers are another. (As for Sales Managers, these are the second most valuable people in the company, next to the CEO; see Chapters 15 and 16).

Top sales reps are the hired guns in a wild west town. Managers are the town's politicians, store managers, stock clerks or sheriff's deputies, depending on their position in the company. Managers comprise a vital part of the work force. Business cannot do without them. Like Barney Fife in *The Andy Griffith Show*, someone has to sit in the sheriff's office, shuffle the wanted posters and be politically correct. Mediocrity isn't bad; but it isn't excellence and high achievers will not tolerate anything less.

I have a hard time dealing with anything less than excellence, and you probably do, too. Most people who put 100% of themselves into what they do have difficulty relating to those who put in 50–60%. Those of us who only get paid when we win our combat in the field have trouble associating with those whose compensation is not based on productivity—those who are paid the same whether they succeed or fail. Yet for some reason, American Business believes that the key to success is through management. For this reason books, tapes and seminars abound in order to help managers manage better, while companies hire so many of them that one day they wake up to the fact that they're top heavy. Then somebody yells, "Downsizing!" and the personnel exodus looks like a Raid® bug spray commercial.

These guys are OK, but the problem is, too often middle managers believe their value is higher than top producing sales reps. It's like some second lieutenant just out of officer training school thinking he or she is superior to a Senior Master Sergeant whose eighteen stripes decorate sleeves he's worn through combat for twenty years. The facts are, good managers make less money and have less freedom than good sales reps. The bottom line is they occupy positions that do not produce revenue for the company. It is for these reasons managers are often uncomfortable with sales reps.

Hey, some of my best friends are managers. They have secretaries who screen calls, type letters, schedule meetings and remember forgotten anniversaries. Top producers should have the same kind of support. Sales assistants can write up orders, schedule calls, send out pertinent sales materials and perform other time-consuming tasks that lead to sales but do not close them. Though a few progressive companies provide this, those still making fire with flint and steel do not.

The most effective hired guns are the ones who are best at the job closest to completing the assignment, i.e.: making the kill, e.g.: closing the deal. Therefore, the more time these excellers have available to perform this top-end function, the more revenue they produce for the company.

The key question to answer in delegating: Can someone less valuable do it?
—*Law of the Hired Gun*

Another difference between excellers and managers is that excellers often hire support people out of their own pockets. I've paid people from outside the company many times to perform lower priority but necessary tasks in correspondence, prospecting and production of sales materials when the company wouldn't step up to the pump. Did the funds for this come out of some departmental budget? Surely you jest. How many managers or VP's have you seen do the same?

Executive O.J.T.

If you're an executive who can't sell water in the desert, that's OK. You weren't hired to sell. But if you're vainglorious enough to think that you can lead a squad of battle-hardened warriors without having any combat experience yourself, you've got another think coming. You'd best get out in the field PDQ—and often. I've never known a sales rep who didn't substantially increase his or her respect for an executive who asked to ride out on calls to witness adversities faced by the sales staff in the field.

**Do not let yourself become a victim
of the circumstances.
Live independent of the circumstances.**

—Law of the Hired Gun

MEMO TO MANAGERS

To: Mr./Ms. MBA
From: The Hired Gun
RE: Staff Prima Donnas

*S*ee those prima donnas you complain about so much? Those hot dogs in their fashion-book clothes and gleaming cars? They're result-oriented, not process oriented. They're not politically correct, and I've got news for you; they're not going to be. You call it arrogance; they call it attitude.

You say you resent flamboyant sales reps? Well I've got more news for you, pilgrim. You're not out in the jungle projecting a successful image of your company for its life or death. Top producers look like a million bucks because they're getting clients to sign contracts for that amount, and because they're worth a lot more to the company than that amount. They're well-groomed, well-dressed, drive high-toned cars. These are the tools of their trade. When clients make decisions to spend their company's money for something new, different or both they put themselves in positions of high-risk. They need to feel confidence in the person who asks them to buy, and every advantage sales reps can show, from intelligent elocution to the shine on their shoes, counts.

> ## Attitude is an outer expression of an inner feeling.
> —*Law of The Hired Gun*
>
>

Who Pays The Piper?

You see, Mr./Ms. Manager, it isn't your company that pays your sales reps; it's your company's clients. Without their money the sales rep doesn't get paid, and neither do you. Those arrogant prima donnas make it happen for everyone.

Overcoming Negative Conditioning

They bust their asses doing the things we were all taught not to do. This is because they've overcome childhoods of negative conditioning put upon them by parents and other adults in our society. I can ask a general audience anywhere in the U.S. if they've heard the following expressions as they grew up and they'll finish the phrases before I do:

> Don't go where you're—not wanted.
> Don't talk to—strangers.
> Don't speak—before being spoken to.
> Don't trust—strangers.
> Don't take people at—their word.

We all grew up hearing these things repeated so many times they've become part of our subconscious. These conditioning statements may have been valuable when we were three and four years old, but not any more. When we're old enough to give our lives defending our country we need to make our own decisions about these things. The problem is, most people never overcome the repeated recordings of these messages in their minds. Thus they live lives of fear: fear of rejection, fear of failure, fear of the unknown.

HEY!

We're born with only two fears: fear of falling and fear of loud noises. All other fears are learned, and we all learned the same ones. We can also get over them.

> **If you keep doing the same thing you will get the same results. If you do more of it, you get more of the same. If you want to change your results, change what you're doing.**
> —*Law of The Hired Gun*

The difference between top sales reps and everyone else is somewhere along the way sales reps learn that negative conditioning statements are mostly products of childhood training. They're behavior checks taught to us for protection when we couldn't be responsible for ourselves. What sales reps learn that others don't is how to overcome them.

If you're going to improve, you need to change something, and the first thing you need to change is the way you see yourself. There are exercises in this book that help you do that. Then you need to change other thoughts about yourself and your surroundings. A list of suggested reading in the back will help you with this. When you change your thoughts, you change your actions. When you change your actions, you change your life. This puts you in control of yourself and your future.

Reprogramming of this magnitude provides salespeople with inner feelings of confidence. This fuels them to make three to four in-person calls or sixty-five to a hundred dials of the phone every day. They do this while middle managers hold monotonous meetings behind the closed doors of their ivory towers, or while executives take three-hour lunches, often figuring how to screw with the sales staff's commissions, divide their territories, raise their quotas or somehow penalize them for doing a good job.

Message To Managers Everywhere

The sales reps stay with you, Mr./Ms. MBA, and like Eli Wallach in _The Magnificent Seven_, you can't imagine why. I suggest you watch that movie and see how and why a sales dream team is formed, and performs. It isn't about cowboys or gunplay, just as this book isn't about paid assassins—we're all about a code:

HONOR, INTEGRITY, LOYALTY.

Watch that movie; read the next chapter of this book. It may enhance your appreciation of the only group of people in your company that brings in the money to pay you and everyone else, before they mount up and ride away to make somebody else rich—most likely your competition.

THE HIRED GUN

> **High Achievers do not stay in an environment in which they cannot achieve. They go wherever they must to meet their needs for achievement.**
> —*Law of the Hired Gun*

*I*n the film *"The Magnificent Seven"*, Mexican peasant villagers are looted regularly by Eli Wallach and his forty thieves to the point they decide they must do something about it. They decide their only recourse is to hire men good with guns. They send emissaries to a distant town to find them. While there, these emissaries witness the heroic action of Yul Brynner and Steve McQueen defending the burial of an Indian in Boot Hill against the armed protests of bigoted citizens. (A request made and paid for by a goodhearted traveling salesman, by the way). McQueen comes from Tombstone, Brynner has left Dodge City:

> **McQueen:** See any action up there?
> **Brynner:** No. Tombstone?
> **McQueen:** Same. People all settled down.
> **Brynner:** Same all over. *(all driving minivans! ed.)*

The Mexican peasants persuade Brynner to recruit five more of the region's best mercenaries. The pay is a pittance, but to these hired guns it's the job at hand that makes the effort worthwhile. The seven gunmen befriend the Mexican villagers; through violent gunfights they rid the town of the menacing hordes. Then one of the town leaders sells them out to Eli Wallach, who ensnares the seven gunfighters in a treacherous deathtrap. As a boss who appreciates the talents of a fast gun, Wallach honors them for their valor and escorts them to the outskirts of town before returning to deal with the villagers.

The tragic flaw of these heroic characters is their intense devotion to the job, their integrity, their pride. For they return, killing Wallach and most of his henchmen, and four of the seven die. As Wallach expires he glares at Yul Brynner and gasps, "You came back! Why?" Brynner doesn't answer. It would waste his breath. The reason would not be understood by a thief who steals the compensation of those who work honestly in the field.

Horst Buchholz: Villages like this make up a song about every big thing that happens.

Brynner: Do you think it's worth it?

Buchholz: Do you?

Brynner: It's only a matter of knowing how to shoot a gun. Nothing big about that.

Buchholz: Hey, how can you talk like this? Your gun has got you everything you have. Isn't it true?

McQueen: (interjecting) Sure, everything. After awhile, you can call bartenders and faro dealers by their first name. Maybe 200 of them; rented rooms you live in, 500; meals you eat in hash houses, 1,000. Home, none. Wife, none. Kids, none. Prospects, zero. S'pose I left anything out?

Brynner: Yes. Places you are tied down to, none. People with a hold on you, none. Men you step aside for, none.

Robert Vaughn: Insults swallowed, none. Enemies, none.

Brynner: No enemies?

Vaughn: None alive.

Buchholz: This is the kind of arithmetic I like!

Brynner: Yes, so did I at your age . . .

(It is commonly known that this western classic is based on Akira Kurosawa's film, "The Seven Samurai," but not many are aware that Kurosawa personally presented director John Sturges a Japanese sword as testament to his fine job with the American film.)

Practical Application

Look at this town as a business beyond despair. Under its own power it barely produces enough to pay the bills and keep its doors open. Every quarter, vulture capitalists bleed its revenues for their greedy self-interests and increase their percentage ownership, leaving the company so destitute it can barely make payroll. The company executives send out recruiters to find sales reps who can produce enough revenue to keep the vultures away.

They get lucky and find seven sales reps of incredible talent. Though the faltering business cannot afford to pay the new reps what they're worth, the sales team shares an esprit de corps of pride, honor and integrity. They offer their services for straight commissions and fair shares of the company's future, based on performance.

Their initial efforts are immediately successful. The company produces more revenue than ever and the parasitic financial backers are forced to leave it alone. But then the CFO sells them out to the vulture capitalists. In a ferocious battle of boardroom tactics, the vultures overrule the Common Stock held by the seven sales reps and the company's officers by invoking their Preferred Stock. They fire four of the reps and withhold their earnings; the other three quit. I've seen it happen.

THE MAN WHO SHOT LIBERTY VALENCE:
But the point of a gun
Was the only law that Liberty understood . . .
When it came to shooting straight and fast
A lawbook was no good."
—*Gene Pitney*

In "Liberty Valence", Jimmy Stewart plays a renowned U.S. Senator and former Ambassador to the Court of St. James. He and his wife arrive on an old steam-powered train, unannounced, to the peaceful western town of Shinbone. They return to pay their respects at a man's funeral, but nobody in town, not even the hounding newspaper editor, has any record of the deceased's existence.

Why does such a popular man return for the funeral of an unknown? Because the *persona non grata corpus delicti* is John Wayne, the only one who kept the town safe from the ravages of Lee Marvin and his lackeys in the old days. Marvin plays the personification of evil as Liberty Valence. He holds up the stage and horsewhips Stewart within an inch of his life because the greenhorn dared defy him in standing up for a lady. Andy Devine, the town's pitiful excuse for a marshal, cowers at the notion of dealing with the badman.

Liberty Valence is evil, wicked, mean and nasty—and as John Wayne says, "He's the toughest man south of the picket wire—next to me." Wayne repeatedly faces Valence, issues challenges that would legitimately allow him to terminate the vermin with maximum prejudice. But evil slithers away when faced by an equal force of good, and so does Liberty Valence.

Finally, Jimmy Stewart unwittingly provides Wayne with the opportunity to eliminate Valence when the outlaw challenges Stewart to a showdown. Stewart, a fledgling attorney who doesn't know the breech of a gun from the barrel, meets Valence in the street while still wearing his dishwasher's apron from the cafe. He knows he's no match for Valence, but courageously faces him anyway. Still, at this point, if the welfare of the town depended on Stewart it would have been raped, pillaged and burned.

Even though drunk, Marvin easily and cruelly wounds Stewart; but just before he can put one "right between the eyes" the Duke blasts him from the shadows with a rifle as Stewart's gun goes off into the dirt. End of story—or is it?

John Wayne is extremely popular as long as Liberty Valence threatens the town. It's only his strength and his gun that holds the evil at bay.

But as soon as Valence dies the girl falls for the wounded dishwasher, the town elects Stewart as a delegate to represent the territory for statehood, and the one who makes it all possible is forgotten, to die unknown.

Reality Check

Let's re-cast Liberty Valence as the wolf at the door of a new business. While he's able to run wild the business isn't secure. We'll make John Wayne the sales force. Security comes in the form of the revenue he provides; it's all that keeps the wolf at bay. Jimmy Stewart co-stars as the politically correct corporate politician. His success occurs only after the wolf is eliminated by long-term sales revenues. Once the company evolves from the entrepreneurial stage to the management stage, salespeople aren't as vital any more. As a matter of fact, they become expendable. The strong ones (the wrong ones) are fired; important deals are taken as house accounts. After awhile, nobody remembers the sales reps who bought the company's stability with their courageous production.

Courageous? Certainly—they could just as easily toil for nothing with an unknown company and its unproved product or service.

John Wayne's presence is vital to the town's early survival, but he's too strong for a society that becomes civilized. Are there similarities between this and you and your company? Do you bring in the money to keep it a safe place to work for everyone else? Prepare yourself for predictable future developments, and feel good about yourself. You are the hero.

Dirty Harry

Only one man on the entire San Francisco police force can nail an insane killer who stalks the streets killing innocent women and children at random. Clint Eastwood's Harry Callahan is an outcast because he doesn't conform to the book, yet whenever there's a dirty job that must get done nobody else has the mettle for it. Whom do they call? The man with the big gun.

Callahan battles departmental politics as much as he fights against the killer, and only persistence, determination, singleness of purpose and a fast powerful gun enable him to bring the killer down. In the final scene of the film the madman holds an innocent boy hostage with a gun to his head. Harry goes against the book, quick-draws and saves the boy's life by blasting the psychopath.

But he knows he'll be chastised for his methods, for his belief in himself and his abilities. According to procedures he should not jeopardize the boy's life by taking his best shot. He should be mediocre like the majority for whom the rules are written. Of course if he weren't Dirty Harry, he would drop his gun, try to negotiate. The boy would be killed and so would he. Harry knows the trials he will face for being different, excellent, successful. He's had enough of petty politics and flings his badge in a lake.

Uncivil Obedience

Cash flow generated by a successful sales force is the only thing that stands between a company's happy shareholders and the bankruptcy court. But have you ever found yourself fighting your company's amnesia with regard to this fact? It's amazing how frequently Alzheimer's Disease creeps into a company's mindset once steady cash flow is obtained. Have you ever had to work as hard selling a deal to your own company as you had to work selling the prospective client? You know the scenario—after you've sold it they don't know if they want to accept it. They actually give you a hard time about it. Perhaps you've had thoughts about flinging your badge in the lake, too.

WHY NOT DO IT, JUST ONCE?

No, I don't mean quit. Dirty Harry didn't quit; look at all the sequels Eastwood made . . . but someday you may just have to agree with management. That deal must be bad. Crumple it up and throw it away, right in front of them.

I can see the outrage on your face now. "Throw it away? But it took a lot of time and hard work to sell it! And it's worth a lot of money . . ."

Wait a minute; you're charged with the responsibility of selling, but do you have the authority? It doesn't sound like it. And the deal isn't worth a wooden nickel if the company doesn't accept it. 100% of nothing is nothing. Authority doesn't come cheap; sometimes you need to sacrifice to earn it. Besides, if the deal is valuable enough you won't get out the door before they dive into the trash can after that contract.

Think about it. Here you are with a contract for $100,000 or $1,000,000 or whatever is relatively high in your industry and some joker is giving you a hard time about accepting it (i.e.: paying you for it) because you sold it during Lent and your company swore off closing deals, or it doesn't have the Pope's approval or the moon was in the wrong house of the zodiac when it was written.

OK, agree with them. Diplomatically tell them you're sorry; they must be right. Then throw it away and leave.

I hope you never have to do this; but if you ever do, you'll only have to do it once. Passive aggressive? No; they're telling you they don't want to accept the deal, you're just making it easier for them. By politely canceling the deal yourself you're absolving them of the angst of having to do it themselves. You're keeping them from the pangs of guilt they'll feel when they bank the client's check with all the zeroes on it and pay you the commission you earn from it. Now, don't you feel better?

When in doubt, look for the financial incentive.

—*Law of The Hired Gun*

Believe me, they're bluffing. They're not arguing the deal; they're arguing paying you for it. If you really want to play hardball, tear it up. The odds are you'll never finish tearing the page because the bottom line is, even if ten to fifteen percent goes to you, the rest goes to the house, and if the house is that stupid, it's time to move on anyway.

Bond, James Bond

Bond—James Bond is the single-most successful movie franchise in the history of film. Bond's loyalty is unparalleled; he always gets results, for Britain and The Queen. He respects his "M"anager and carries the respect of same. But even in this famous series, there are times when Bond resigns (On Her Majesty's Secret Service and License To Kill) to go his own way, to live by his personal code of honor. It is Bond's indefatigable resilience, confidence, independence and sense of humor in the face of death that makes him indestructible—the ultimate hired gun.

It's interesting that in Goldeneye the new Ms. M is referred to as "the evil queen of numbers, a beancounter" who chastises Bond for being a "sexist, misogynist dinosaur; a relic of the Cold War." In that movie it's a good thing one of these misplaced creatures still roams the earth, otherwise the world is toast.

Yes, by comparison many top producers are seen as arrogant, overpaid, flamboyant, uncontrollable. But who does the company run to when a client worth millions of dollars leaves? On whom do they depend to replace that revenue? Quit smirking.

One Riot, One Ranger

The Hired Gun Syndrome does not just occur in fiction, rather the fictions are reflections of facts; witness:

A town in west Texas was ravaged by mob violence. The mayor sent a telegram to the governor to rush a force of Texas Rangers to help.

The train finally arrived and a citizens committee turned out to meet the Rangers, but only one stepped from the train. Captain Bill McDonald of Company B was alone, leather-skinned and keen-eyed. The citizens protested his inadequacy to control the violence, and the mayor asked, "Why did the governor only send one Ranger?" "Well," he said, "you ain't got but one riot, have you?"

That's all it used to require. The Texas Rangers have one of the most distinguished records in the annals of crimefighting. No other state has an equivalent to them, an outfit that dates back over 170 years to ten men who were hired by Stephen F. Austin to protect settlers from Indians. This duty grew to include bandits, bank robbers, bootleggers, lynch mobs, labor disputes and serial killers. In those days of desperados, results were all that mattered, and it was Texas Rangers who brought down such infamous killers as Sam Bass and Bonnie and Clyde, among others.

The Texas Rangers were led by men who stressed individuality, independence and results. They were expected not to burden the Captains with details, but to go where they were needed and work until the job was finished. If they needed help, they had a direct line to the Colonel, The Boss of the entire outfit. These were men who had to live off the land, go through numerous days of sleepless pursuit, fight mobs, overpower killers on the open range.

But today's rules are different. Bad guys aren't bad guys anymore; they're victims of dysfunctional families, temporary insanity or racism and poverty. Crooks don't serve time in the Big House anymore; they walk the streets after repeated offenses to commit more crimes. Today's Rangers face increasing difficulties performing to the level of excellence that is their legend. This is not due to inability to apprehend criminals, but to being overrun by bleeding heart rights advocates.

New quotas force the hiring of applicants, based not on merit but on race and sex, to fill the elite ranks of eighty-seven Rangers with desk clerks, officers with experience limited to the driver's license service and relatives of politicians. Another hindrance to their legendary devotion to duty are recent federal labor regulations that limit the hours that can be worked. A Ranger quoted in *Texas Monthly* in February 1995 said, "I remember they forced me to take off twenty straight days because I had worked too many hours . . . It was ridiculous, and it brought a hardship on the rural counties that depended on me to work their cases." The author of the article wrote, "The Texas Rangers had now become politically correct and were the worse for it." Consequently, in recent years many veteran Rangers have turned in their badges.

In the rootin' tootin' days of a new enterprise, the sales force is a band of Rangers. It's small, elite and territories are broad. Training is minimal. Reps are hired for their proven experience and expected to get the job done without a lot of hand-holding or mollycoddling. Independence and individuality is rewarded. But at the point that cash flow becomes somewhat steady, the corporate politicians move in. Suddenly there are rules and procedures, approval processes, layers of management between you and The Boss.

You need to be aware of this. The only thing constant in life is change. When your company changes around you, you'll need to make one of two choices, just like modern day Rangers:

1) adapt and overcome.

2) leave.

This is not an easy decision. It involves your emotions as much or more than your rationale. But the bottom line is binary; it's black or white. You either stay or go. Best to make this decision for yourself before it's made for you.

How To Know When It's Time To Go

1) You're not rewarded enough for your work: whether money, respect, benefits or recognition.

2) Advancement is blocked: family-owned business populated by in-laws? New ownership staffing up with its own people?

3) Management is poor—If you lack confidence and/or respect for your leadership go somewhere you'll be proud to work.

4) You're not excited by what you do: Without a passion for what you're selling, you won't perform up to your own expectations.

5) You've turned off your dream machine: If you know in your gut that there's a dream you should pursue—go for it!

The Great Equalizer

Sales, like the old Colt .45 Peacemaker, is the modern day equalizer. Samuel Colt developed the Colt-Walker six-shooter specifically for the Texas Rangers. When the gun was issued it was said, "The Lord made some men big; the Lord made some men small. Samuel Colt made them equal." In sales, unlike most other jobs, modern day employment issues of race, sex, religious beliefs and nepotism vanish. Whereas managers, accountants, production staff and executives are sometimes hired without qualification and too often retained after proving incompetent, in sales the only thing that counts is production. As long as you can sell you can make money anywhere you go; but if you can't close a door, it doesn't matter whose friend you are, you're history.

Let's examine one last historical example:

SIR WINSTON CHURCHILL

After the fiasco of Nevil Chamberlain's kinder gentler division of Czechoslovakia with Hitler, Parliament brought in Churchill at age sixty-five to be Prime Minister. A person whose life had been checkered with ups and downs, he believed it was all to prepare him for this turbulent task and looked upon it as a matter of destiny. Indeed, a logical man would have surrendered, but an impulsive man, a man of action was prepared to meet a seemingly unbeatable enemy in the Nazis.

Only the English Channel separated a pitifully unprepared Britain from the invincible Nazi Army. The world waited for England to surrender, but they had not figured on the character of the man who had been successful, failed, come back, and come back again. Churchill's character was that of a man who never surrendered, and it came through in his famous words that inspired the British people when nothing else could:

> **"WE SHALL DEFEND OUR ISLAND, WHATEVER THE COST MAY BE. WE SHALL FIGHT ON THE BEACHES, WE SHALL FIGHT ON THE LANDING GROUNDS, WE SHALL FIGHT IN THE FIELDS, AND IN THE STREETS, WHATEVER THE COST MAY BE. WE SHALL NOT SURRENDER."**

During the Battle of Britain, Nazi bombers blasted London, but Churchill imbued England with courage throughout those harrowing fifty-seven nights. He didn't just speak, he took action, out amongst the people on the streets and in the shelters.

> **". . . IF THE BRITISH EMPIRE AND ITS COMMONWEALTH LASTS FOR A THOUSAND YEARS, MEN WILL STILL SAY THIS WAS THEIR FINEST HOUR."**

After seven years of war, Churchill's Britain survived the greatest threat in its history. But only two months after V.E. day, England saw its hero as a man of war who was no longer needed in times of peace, and *voted him out of office.*

"Sales beats marketing."

Tom Peters makes an interesting comment in an article he contributed to Forbes ASAP entitled, "Of Things Fundamental." In it, he discusses the notion that, "there's nothing like a crazy startup to remind you of the basics, something no gazillion-dollar firm can ever do." In helping a friend set up his new business, Peters makes this conclusive assessment regarding a start-up operation:

" . . . it's become clear to my pal and me that sales comes first. There's no bonanza for the world's greatest widget until there's a completed connection with the customer . . . we require a driven, proven national-account sales genius to get us going with a bang. We began by thinking we needed an inspired marketer, with some sales background. Now we are convinced we need an inspired salesperson—with some marketing history." He continues with, "the 'job' must be a labor of passion, not a day at the office or a bullet point for the resume."

Believe In Yourself

You have a choice; you're a sales rep. There are always companies like the one in Peters' example clamoring to find a Hired Gun to get things going and willing to pay a handsome price for this most important talent. This is the scenario that we look for, that we thrive in: newness, leading edge, enthusiasm, genuine input, passion for achievement. It's also where you can:

> **Make as much as you can, as fast as you can, as long as you can.**
> —Law of The Hired Gun

The point is, you are not alone in doing a remarkable job, then determining that it's time to move on, or having that decided for you. In both fiction and fact many of the world's great heroes have had it happen to them. When the streets are lawless, as in the entrepreneurial growth stage of a new business, everybody wants you on their side. They need you; you're essential to their survival. But once it gets civilized, rules, regulations and procedures are given more importance than results. When process outranks results it's time to saddle up and move on.

Be loyal to your Boss and your job, but keep that résumé updated. The characteristics that will keep you successful over the life of your career aren't just closing ability, making effective presentations or overcoming objections. They are being resilient, adaptable, indestructible.

WHENEVER YOU FEEL LUCKY, DRAW!

emember the old arcade game with the masked quick-draw bandit? You strapped on an electronic six-shooter and faced him as he issued pre-recorded arrogant taunts. You drew against each other and if he won, he gave you a mocking laugh.

Well slap leather, pilgrim. Let's see what kind of Hired Gun you are. This quiz is designed to help you identify your position among Top Guns, with a wee bit of editorial on faux pas practices we endure daily. HINT:

> **If you're not on the cutting edge, you're taking up too much space.**
> —*Law of The Hired Gun*

1. My ideal sales opportunity is:
   - a. An established company with a lot of benefits.
   - b. A new company with unique products/concepts.
   - c. The one I've been selling for the past decade.
   - d. Being with a group of salespeople I like.
2. If I had my druthers, I'd be compensated by:
   - a. Salary, so I'm secure.
   - b. Straight commission, so I'm free.
   - c. Draw against commission, so I know I've got something coming.
   - d. Guaranteed base plus commission, so I can't fail.

3. Annually, I need to earn:

        a. Over $150,000.

        b. Over $100,000.

        c. Over $ 70,000.

        d. Over $ 50,000.

4. In a sales situation I:

        a. Don't have to think about what I'm doing.

        b. Know that I know what I'm doing.

        c. Know that I don't know what I'm doing.

        d. Don't even know that I don't know what I'm doing.

5. It's been a strong hard month of sales. After the last day is over, I:

        a. Want to go home and be left alone.

        b. Go to a bar to celebrate with friends.

        c. Go to a movie for some mindless entertainment.

        d. Take my date/spouse out to a fine dinner.

6. I feel successful in my sales position because of the:

        a. Money I make.

        b. Trips and awards I win.

        c. Friendships I have with my colleagues at work.

        d. Years I have with the company.

7. In terms of goals, I

        a. Write my goals and measure my development.

        b. Took a break. A goal to get where I am would have been unrealistic.

        c. Have some goals in mind.

        d. Make a resolution every New Year's Eve.

8. My selling skills are:

        a. As good as they can possibly be.

        b. Excellent, but I'm always looking for ways to sharpen my skills.

        c. Good enough to get by.

        d. Not where I'd like to be, but I'm learning as fast as I can.

9. My future professional aspiration is to:

    a. Conceive and build my own business.

    b. Be a corporate executive.

    c. Be a manger of salespeople.

    d. Make enough selling so I can retire young to Spain's Costa del Sol.

10. When The Boss asks to see me in his/her office, I:

    a. Start packing up my office.

    b. Get my numbers together to defend my performance.

    c. Try to control my swagger and grin when I walk in.

    d. Poll my friends, "what's up?" before going.

11. When I sense that the person leaning in my doorway with a coffee cup in their hand is looking for someone to meet their need for affiliation on the company's time, I:

    a. Walk with them to the coffee machine so we can find some others.

    b. Ask how they're doing and offer them a chair.

    c. Quickly pick up the phone and dial the call I'm scheduled to make.

    d. Tell them I'd like to talk, but ask if it can be later.

12. When sales managers say they want to go out on calls with me, I:

    a. Scramble to set up meetings with existing clients.

    b. Ask if they can handle six appointments tomorrow.

    c. Wish they'd go with someone else so they don't blow my sale.

    d. Look forward to their help.

    e. Fear they'll see something about me they don't like.

13. A colleague I respect asks if I'll help on a deal they're trying to close. I:

    a. Wish they'd go ask somebody else. I'm busy with my own deals.

    b. Hope I live up to their expectations. I'll do whatever I can to help.

    c. Begrudgingly accept, as long as it's convenient to me.

    d. Think up an excuse not to. I may respect them, but I'm not going to help them beat my numbers.

14. I know it was a good day because I:

    a. Got an At-A-Boy from The Boss.

    b. Got my paycheck.

    c. Closed a deal.

    d. Had a great lunch with my friends.

15. Frequent meetings are:

    a. A necessary evil of the job.

    b. Something that should be done in memos, instead.

    c. To be avoided if at all possible.

    d. Necessary for effective communications.

    e. Required, and darned well should be.

16. In terms of tenure at my company, I:

    a. Owe my life to this company.

    b. Was looking for a job when I found this one.

    c. Have a great position, but keep my eyes open for other opportunities.

    d. Will have to write them a check to work here if they don't stop charging me back on my deals.

17. When headhunters contact me with opportunities I:

    a: Tell them I owe my life to the company.

    b. Jump at the chance to get another job.

    c. Stress my loyalty, tell them I'm doing well, but let them know I'll look if the opportunity warrants it.

    d. Ask how they got my name.

18. When I'm at a party and someone asks me what I do, I tell them:

    a. A good joke.

    b. I'm in sales.

    c. The name of the company I work for.

    d. Nothing. I ask what they do.

19. Strictly as a human being—as opposed to a professional, a par-

ent, a club member, or a friend—strictly as a person on a scale of zero to ten, ten being high, I rate:

    a. 10
    b. 8
    c. 6
    d. 5 or less

20. When I go on vacation, I go:

    a. Anywhere in the world.
    b. Anywhere in the U.S.
    c. 75 miles to my lake house, and 75 miles back.
    d. To the local bar every day at 5:00.

Answers:

1. If you want to play it safe, get a job with the government as a civil servant. They have lots of benefits, you can stay there forever without getting fired, and you'll make lots of friends on coffee breaks and lunch hours. [a=2, b=5, c=3, d=1]

2. The government pays salaries, too. Even if you totally screw up, you still make the same amount of money. The more secure you are on the bottom by some base or draw, the less you can earn in the top end by producing excellent results. [a=0, b=5, c=4, d=2]

3. Even in a job selling widgets on the street, a Top Gun can earn plenty of money. If you're good but caught in a business where earning potential is low, look for new waters to jump in and swim. [a=5, b=4, c=3, d=2]

4. Practiced professionals don't have to think about what they do before the motions come to them; they've done it so many times it's automatic. They shoot from the hip with confidence—and hit the target

(Unconscious Competent). Talented amateurs take time to think, make sure what they're doing is right, then make their move (Conscious Competent). Rookies are aware that they have a lot to learn (Conscious Incompetent). Pinheads are so clueless that they don't even know that they don't know what they're doing (Unconscious Incompetent). [a=5, b=4, c=3, d= -1]

5. Though salespeople tend to be naturally gregarious, after we've interacted with fifty to a hundred people a day for twenty-five work days in a month we often just need some self-time. If we're in a good personal relationship, we want to spend our available time with that other significant person in our lives. Or we just want a mental massage or a good drink. 5 points for any answer to this one, with an extra five if you chose them all. (Nobody said you could only choose one answer!)

6. The company didn't offer a lucrative opportunity to you so you could make friends. If you feel successful due to length of time in the job, you're probably operating in the ether of a comfort zone. The more you produce the more money you make. You can pay for your own trips in first class, rather than in the economy coach and tourist hotels most awards provide. [a=5, b=3, c=1, d=1]

7. Yes, the difference between the most successful people in the world and those who aspire to be successful are written, specific goals. But the truly flamboyant semi-arrogant person, who always comes out on top no matter what, is such an unconscious competent that setting goals for income or production sometimes becomes an exercise in futility. If I had set a goal to earn as much as the top producer at most other divisions in my telemarketing company, I would have earned $100,000 a year less than I did. Tripling this was attained by simply doing everything I possibly could to realize the maxim of "Make as much as you can, as fast as you can." A goal to triple the production of the other company leaders would not have been realistic, and anything less would have been self-limiting. [a=5, b=5, c=1, d=0]

8. No matter how much of a prima donna you are, how much experience you have, how much money you make, you can always benefit from others and learn new skills. If you're only trying to get by, congratulations on your decision to live in mediocrity. [a=1, b=5, c=1, d=4]

9. Selling may be a blast, it may be exciting, and it is certainly rewarding. But let's face it, it's a rat race of high anxiety and stress. That's why it pays so well. It's not unlike gambling. We want to take the house down and get out as winners. It's certainly admirable to desire to build your own operation and be another statistical Boss with a sales background, and Lord knows that any sales force that gets a sales manager who has a career of consistent high production is blessed. But score this one as follows: [a=4, b=2, c=3, d=5]

10. If you're doing everything you can to do the best job you can, you should have nothing to fear, especially from The Boss. If your numbers aren't up, The Boss probably just wants to ask if there's anything that can be done to help sales. My experience is that people who are about to be fired already know why they're getting called in. And if you've just put up record numbers for the fifth month in a row, try not to swagger too much. [a= -1, b=1, c=5, d=3]

11. You didn't get where you are in sales by leaning in a doorway with a U.S. government coffee cup in your hands, or by taking Dr Pepper breaks at 10, 2 and 4. It's kind of rude to jump on the phone as soon as a colleague walks in, so be diplomatic and let someone know that you're a professional, even if they're not. [a=1, b=1, c=3, d=5.]

12. When sales managers want to go out on calls with you, it's probably so they can see if there is something they can pass along to other salespeople to help them out. Setting up appointments with existing clients says two things about you: 1) You don't have any appointments in

the first place, and 2) you're so insecure that you only want to take the manager on calls to people who already buy from you. These are both signs of weakness. A new manager went out on calls with me one time and we made six in-person sales calls and did not break for lunch. He was completely gassed at the end of the day. Had I realized his health was not good, I would have sincerely asked if he was up to it, first. I've also had sales managers I wanted to just stay home and do paperwork as they were nothing but detriments in an actual call. [a=0, b=5, c=4, d=4, e=1]

13. An important law of life is the Law of Reciprocity. You get what you give. [a=2, b=5, c=2.5, d=0]

14. An At-A-Boy and fifty cents will get you a cup of coffee (Well, not any more; it's three bucks now.) Your paycheck is for something you've accomplished in the past. Doing The Deal is what it's all about. [a=3, b=2, c=5, d=2]

15. Managers who don't have much to do love to hold meetings so they can feel like they're doing something important. Meetings only keep sales reps away from doing what they're hired and paid to do: sell. [a=3, b=4, c=5, d=2, e=1]

16. This is not your marriage; it's a job. If you need to change something in your life, change jobs before convincing yourself that your job is your life and finding out that your spouse has left. You owe the company your loyalty and the best performance you can give, but your life belongs to God and yourself and your family. [a=3, b=4, c=5, d=2]

17. When you're good, you'll be recruited constantly by professional headhunters or other people who know about your reputation. You don't want to jump jobs too frequently, but neither do you owe your life to the company. Just because you're successful where you are doesn't mean you can't be happier, or more successful somewhere else. Be hon-

orable and maintain your integrity and loyalty, but when viable positions are offered to you be sure to do your homework on them. [a = 2, b = 1, c = 5, d = 3]

18. If you're ashamed to tell people you're in sales, you need to do something else. Cloaking it in the guise of naming your company is hiding, reversing them by asking what they do may seem coy and mysterious, but it's hiding as well. Of course, anybody likes a good joke. [a = 4, b = 5, c = 2, d = 2]

19. If you answered anything other than ten, you're wrong. We all start life as a ten. The only reason we end up feeling less than a ten is because somebody else told us we are. We are born with only two natural fears: fear of falling and fear of loud noises. All other fears are learned. The same goes for our feelings about ourselves. The single most important factor in the success of your life is your self-image, the picture of yourself you carry around with you in everything you do. Every day you take this picture of yourself into the marketplace and you sell yourself for money and a way of life. How much you believe in yourself and how much you put into all the different things you do determines how much money you make, what kind of neighborhood you live in, where your kids go to school. Tens feel good about themselves and are proud of it. Eights want to say they're tens, but are afraid it will sound cocky. Sixes have been told all their lives they're just better than average. Fives (and less) show up for life, punch the time clock, then retire and die. [a=5, b=4, c=2.6, d=1]

20. Excellers take world vacations. Even if money is tight, they figure out a way to go places other people only think about going. High Achievers want to See America, First. Average performers take a 150 mile vacation, seventy-five out and seventy-five back. Anything else is A Trip! Losers are on permanent vacation. [a=5, b=4, c=3, d=0]

Scoring:

95–100: Double-O Section. You should be issued a gold-plated License To Kill. You are confident, committed, loyal, experienced, successful, and secure enough to help others. Any company would do well to add you to its sales team.

90–95: Paladin. "A knight without armor in a savage land." You're an experienced mercenary of sales who can sell anything, anywhere. You have all the talents and abilities to be in the Double-O Section, you're just from a different era.

80–90: The Kid. In the movie about a crack sales team, you're played by Tom Cruise, opposite the more experienced Al Pacino. You have the desire and natural ability to make it to the big time. If an experienced gunfighter teaches you a few important qualities like keeping your cool under fire and the Zen of hitting your target without aiming, you'll be up there with the Double-O's.

70–80: Quick Draw Artist. You're very good, and you can hit the target while looking in a mirror, but lack the killer instinct.

60–70: Sam The Bartender. In Gunsmoke, Sam was a tough guy past his prime who kept a sawed-off shotgun behind the bar. Most of the time he operated in his comfort zone serving drinks, polishing glasses and socializing with the clientele of the Long Branch Saloon. But if he or Miss Kitty was vitally threatened the big gun came out. You have the ability to be a killer sales rep; you just prefer to operate in your comfort zone most of the time.

50–60: Mushy. In the old western series *Rawhide*, Gil Favor was the trail boss, Rowdy Yates (played by Clint Eastwood) was ramrod, Wishbone was the cook, and Mushy—a nice, somewhat simple guy who everybody liked, but who wouldn't kill a deer for food if he was starving to death, was the chuck wagon assistant. He was a great guy, but his role was helping out the drovers . . . You like the interaction with clients and you make a contribution to the overall effort by helping out. This is valuable because you take this burden off the company's big closers. Your mission is to keep the big guns supplied with ammo; just don't slap leather against them.

WRITE YOUR IDENTITY

*P*erforming this exercise sets you apart from 99.99% of the people in the world. Writing your identity isn't easy; in fact, it's hard work. If it was easy, everybody would do it. It involves the most intense introspection you may ever do, but it pays HUGE dividends.

"What Is My Identity?"

Few people know. We're not taught to give it much thought, yet it is the single most important quality we can know about ourselves. Our identity is who we are as human beings, as opposed to the things we do in life. It's our feeling of self-worth, our self-image.

Deep within our soul we carry a picture of ourselves. This picture shows how we see ourselves day in and day out as a person. Every day we get up and take this picture into the marketplace. We use it to sell ourselves for business; we use it to sell ourselves for a way of life. How well we use this determines how much money we make, where we live, what kind of car we drive, where our kids go to school.

If you were to pull this picture out to look at right now, what would it show? Most of us don't know, because we've never stopped to consider it, much less study it, decide to improve upon it and take conscious action on it. Sure, we're often told, "Know thyself!" (Aristotle) but nobody ever tells us how.

This Is How

A common characteristic among the most successful people in the world is this: They continually work to establish, develop and reinforce their identities. If you get nothing more from this entire book than the benefit of this exercise, you must absolutely positively stop right now and write this out. Don't mark it to come back to later. Do it. Do it now. Do it right now. Even if it's just a brainstorm outline of words. Get them down. Get started. There are two other opportunities in this book for you to refine and reinforce this important work, so don't worry about coloring within the lines right now. We're just sketching. You may not be able to paint a picture, but you can write a thousand words. Start here with about a hundred. Do it on the page provided, then tear it out and carry it in your wallet so you can refer to it often, especially when you encounter periods of self-doubt. Remember that these periods are often brought about by someone else. Often their objective is to make you feel less valuable so they can feel better about themselves by pulling you down. Don't let them! Remember who you are; re-read the identity you write.

Premise

When you started out in life your personal value was just as good as anybody else's. On a scale of zero to Ten, as human beings we're all born Tens. The only reason you may not feel like a Ten about yourself as a person is because someone else told you you're less than a Ten—and you believed them. That's OK. You didn't know better, then. You know better now.

As of this moment you can rewrite who you are. Brainstorm; jot down words that come into your mind that describe the kind of person you want to see when you look inside yourself.

Are you: strong, caring, defiant, independent, sharing, giving, attractive, dynamic, honest, gallant, funny, fair, positive? Think about it. There are thousands of words you can use. This is just a start. And it isn't just writing individual adjectives; use them in descriptive sentences about yourself. Believe me, the words you choose are unique. They are because you are, and you choose them.

The problem is most of us have never had the opportunity presented to us or taken the time to sit down and work on—ourselves. Don't be shy. This is an exercise written by you, for you and nobody else but you. It's for your eyes only. To help you get started, here's an example from a friend of mine (It's OK, I have written permission.) It's a bit high-strung, but you can feel his wit together with his intensity:

"I am a high-performance machine. Top performance is my destiny. I drink super-octane methanol and eat solid rocket fuel. My lungs breathe through ram-air induction and my legs say "Firestone" on the side. I blow straight ahead and nothing stops me from hitting my goals. I come from the best genetics, the best education, and I put everything I have into everything I do. I win because I expect to win. This is the way I am. There is no other choice."

Here's another one, a little less aggressive:

"I am confident and strong; well-mannered and considerate of others. I enjoy sophisticated tastes and work to improve my knowledge of art, music, literature and performance. I have been blessed with good feelings and good looks and most especially, good friends. These are important to me and I strive to develop them. I am independent, financially stable and open to making new friends."

Write Your Identity:

_____

_____

_____

_____

_____

_____

_____

_____

_____

MERCENARY OF SALES

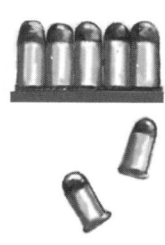

> **I cannot sell something successfully without a passion for its cause.**
> —*Law of The Hired Gun*

How did you come to be in the job you have now? Did you plan it? Specifically seek it? Did it fall from heaven and land in your lap on a silver serving tray? Were you headhunted and recruited to take it? Or was it the first thing available when you needed to make some money? Just for the record, I can answer yes to each of these during different phases of my career.

And why do you do it? Because you believe in the concept of your business? The mission statement of your company? Because you like the people you work with every day? Because of the money? The benefits? Because you've done it for so long now that you wouldn't know what else to do? Because you have a family that depends on you for an income?

There's nothing wrong with any of these. They're all valid for anyone who subscribes to them. Personally, I do what I do for the freedom and the money. In that order. I used to think it was the other way around until the first day I went back into sales out of the straight jacket of sales management. The joy I felt to be out on my own again made it instantly clear that money was not the object—although it does have a way of ranking pretty high up there.

To me the job is a means to an end. I have a mission in my life, just as you do in yours: a lifestyle to lead, dreams to fulfill, things to see, places to go, people to do. But the job I take must be one I believe in as if the company were my own. Without this I would not have the motivation to get to the office first and stay there last, to make more calls than anyone else, and to make each presentation with passionate conviction and belief. I take each job as a commitment for the long haul and swear loyalty to The Boss who makes that opportunity possible. I sell with a vengeance until somebody asks me to stop.

Most people I know have parents and grandparents who did one basic job for one basic company, for their entire careers. You know: the father who started in the international oil company's mail room just out of college and ended up as vice-president of the corporation with a thirty-five year lapel pin given to him by the company president; the uncle who served twenty-two years in the military and retired with a pension, then started a second career in private business; the physician grandfather whose practice spanned four decades in the same town.

The irony is that the descendants of these folks, the people I know today, have rarely been in the same position more than four or five years themselves, me included. Now, we can hang out in a book store until they turn out the lights flipping through sociological studies about planned job changes, colored parachutes, high divorce rates, lack of commitment and short attention spans caused by myriad factors including 120 edits in a thirty second TV commercial. But I'd rather not. Accept the fact that if you were born during or after the Baby Boom the only constant you'll have in your life is change.

 = K.

**Of all the people who will
never leave you,
you're the only one.**
—*Law of The Hired Gun*

Head Games

It was your decision to get into this profession. You consciously chose it and you chose to pay the price for success in it. But you didn't consciously choose to deal with ceaseless efforts by executives to distract your laser beam focus—the intensity essential to your success. You didn't elect to play the head games they constantly create in the form of long-winded meetings that sap your selling time, errant paychecks, revised territories, altered commission plans, manipulated account lists and discontinued spiff plans. Then there are the alleged austerity programs . . . Just for fun, let's take a look at common rationalizations for each of these:

Chargebacks: It has taken you three weeks to satisfy accounting that the money missing from your last paycheck is actually an error made by someone whose salary for a year is less than you make in a month. Management assures you that although the matter wasn't resolved in time for this payroll, it'll be included in your next commission check, a month away. In the meantime, good luck with your bills during that eight week term.

Territory: You've invested years building a good reputation for your company in your area of responsibility, and your territory in particular yields more than any other in the company. Nonetheless, management has decided to get more out of each territory so they're splitting them all and doubling the sales force.

This is how they reward you for doing an excellent job. Of course, you'll have to relinquish some of the accounts on your list for the new rep who's taking over part of your area. Hey, Mother Theresa wouldn't have any problem with it . . .

The Pay Plan: Mediocre sales reps are making too much money from substandard results, so commission rates are being changed, effective immediately. Unfortunately these changes include those of you who have been doing an exemplary job, too. We have to be fair to everybody. (Why?)

Spiffs: Just because spiffs boosted sales for a short time doesn't mean they should continue. (They wouldn't want to continue boosting sales!) Too many salespeople are hooked on "spiff dope" and sell just to make the short term hit, losing sight of long term sales projections. By the way, why are numbers down this month?

Austerity program: Management is cutting back expenses and perqs.

1) "Why?" you ask.

"Due to lagging sales revenues."

2) "What about the record month we produced recently?"

"Costs of sales are too high."

3) "What about the fact that the cost of a salesperson averages only ten to fifteen percent of a sale's revenue?" *

"Well, yes, but the company is expanding."

The Rule of Three:
When you ask someone a question that makes them uncomfortable, give them plenty of time to *finish* answering.

- ◆ **The first thing they say is what they think *they* want to hear.**
- ◆ **The second thing is what they think *you* want to hear.**
- ◆ **The third thing they say is the *truth*.**

—*Law of The Hired Gun*

So the company needs to cut back on the commitments it made to you so it can support growth in other areas (like executives' stock options). The greed of the corporate beast; been there, fought that.

I rarely hear of executives tying their personal salaries directly to the performance of the company. If they make bonehead mistakes that fail to produce revenues and profits, do they take home less pay, like salespeople do if they blow a sale? No. Maybe their stock options indirectly suffer, but that bi-weekly check to pay their bills is never touched, except for the annual raises they receive for being predictable and not making waves.

Why don't sales reps get annual percentage commission increases? Is a sales rep no more valuable after having been with the company for four, five, ten years? Why should a sales rep who has proven loyal to the company for years on end be compensated at exactly the same rate as a brand new person? Are experienced managers compensated the same as newly hired ones? Are any employees with years of seniority paid the same rate as a brand new person? In most sales organizations, the sales reps are all paid the same commission rate, regardless of their experience level.

*Dartnell's 29th Sales Force Compensation Survey 1996-1997 reports the overall cost of sales as a percentage of total sales volume at 12.2%, compared to 10.1 % in 1990.

> **"IT'S THE ORDERS YOU DISOBEY**
> **THAT MAKE YOU FAMOUS."**
> —*General Douglas MacArthur*

HOW I GOT THIS WAY

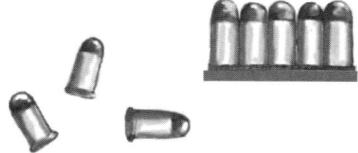

My parents taught me to win... Believe it or not, I started out respectably. Good student, good schools, high SAT's, college scholarship on the conference champion track team at the University of Texas at Austin. My father, a Captain in the U.S. Navy, was its foremost authority on decompression medicine, the second President of the Undersea Medical Society, recipient of the Legion of Merit—highest non-combat medal given in the armed forces. He also received accolades from the Secretary of the Navy, the Japanese Navy, Swedish Navy, French Navy and won the 1964 NOGI Award for Undersea Science over Jacques Cousteau and Scott Carpenter, among others. And my mom is smarter than he is! Though he was valedictorian of his high school class, she was salutatorian of hers, Phi Beta Kappa in college, Master's in Education. My heritage was purely academic, and I was aimed toward authorship of literature with a capital L.

Joe Charbonneau taught me to fast-draw . . . After undergraduate and graduate degrees, my first paid position was indeed in writing—sales training literature. I didn't know much about sales, but didn't need to. The research was already compiled, handed to me in well organized stacks by the man who became my mentor in success, Joe Charbonneau.

Joe had a dream of creating sales and management training seminars and programs that really worked, not just a bunch of tapes that would sell and gather dust on someone's shelves. He produced systems that delivered predictable, desirable, measurable results in self-image and performance improvement and needed someone to write them. I took the job and became immersed in the world of sales: the ability to help someone get something that benefits them, the honesty of a transaction, the art of persuasion, the creation of a strong self-image. I was hooked.

During the next four years I worked twelve hours a day, six days a week learning everything I could about how to sell, how to succeed, how to train others to do the same. I made good money for the time, but that wasn't the issue. I received an incredible apprenticeship in sales and business available to very few people. Those who received similar lessons from Joe paid fortunes to take seminars and learn what I was paid to experience all day, every day, six and a half days a week.

After about three years Joe called me into his office one day, looked me straight in the eyes and grinned. "You have no way of knowing," he said, "but by the time you're thirty, you're going to be absolutely illegal." I wasn't very good at handling compliments, they embarrassed me, and this one rolled off my back as another of Joe's sincere attempts to make me feel valuable to the organization. I should have known better—Joe is almost always right.

My jobs gave me guns and bullets . . . A few years later I took my skills to another business. Leaving Joe's company was one of the most difficult decisions I've ever made. This was the man who taught me everything from keeping a neat briefcase to determining a decision-maker's needs for power, achievement or affiliation in order to close the deal.

I employed several decision-making processes: listed benefits and detriments on separate sheets of paper, talked with friends, talked with Joe. At first, I thought that several years of twelve hour days and six day weeks that compressed six weeks into every month had burned me out. That was the first Rule of Three. Then I told myself that every student needs to leave the master. That was the Second Rule. I wanted to start applying all that I'd learned; I itched to get out there on my own. That was the truth.

My wife clipped an ad from the classifieds and laid it on my dresser—a new outfit with an experimental concept in advertising needed seven high-powered sales reps. Hundreds interviewed for the few positions offered, and somehow I got the last one. The sales manager referred to me as his dark horse. I was so excited I drove ninety m.p.h. all the way home before I noticed the speedometer.

Kings of Junk Mail

Dallas was a test market for a new concept of mailing printed ads in bundles, like in newspapers. But instead of being limited to the average 30% market penetration of that Gutenberg-era medium, our company's saturation mail program hit virtually 100% of the market's mailboxes on a weekly basis.

What really made the program fly was a sales manager who put together a team every bit as good as Yul Brynner's band of movie mercenaries. In terms of experience and ability, I rated myself in the lower portion of the lower half of the group. I've been in sales for decades since and have never seen the quality and energy I found in these colleagues.

Within a few hyper-intensive months we grew from a fledgling concept to a serious threat to local newspapers. There were only seven of us against scores of reps on three major dailies that had been entrenched for a century, yet we seriously invaded their revenues, won clients and signed advertising contracts for hundreds of thousands of dollars. We made pretty good money, too. That's when Roy the Boy, one of the sales reps, stumbled on the plan to cut commissions.

Musketeer Mentality

I washed up one evening after feeding the horses on my ranchette when I took a phone call in the kitchen. I was told my colleagues called a meeting the next day at lunch, and it was vital that I be there. Just sales; no managers.

The next day I learned over my enchiladas that Roy the Boy made an interesting discovery when he worked late the previous night. While turning in sales orders for the next week he stumbled across plans to reduce our commissions by 25% initially, and even more as sales increased.

Sales reps tend to be conservative. The very nature of our occupation makes us proponents of the free enterprise system. We also tend to be independent. Consequently, we tend toward a right-to-work mentality and would never consider group actions against our own company.

In this case, however, we knew that the only leverage we had to stop this foolish attack on our earnings was to stand together. We had all the clients and all the orders. The program was just getting off the ground. We knew this was the one moment we could successfully hold their feet to the fire, and we did. All for one and one for all. After we agreed to hang together, we invited the would-be cutthroat to our luncheon.

When he arrived, a bit perplexed, we informed him that there was only one source of revenue supporting this endeavor, and he was looking at it. Either we reached an immediate agreement to solidify the commissions we had been promised upon hiring, or no business would be turned in. Cash flow would halt. It would take months to replace our efforts. The operation would die.

Our point was simple. A deal is a deal. We kept our commissions.

Here we go again . . .

A year later a Lilliputian H.O.E. (Home Office Executive) in the HQ tried a more subtle end-around play to reduce sales commissions. He retained the services of an allegedly independent consulting group to interview personnel, analyze pay structures and make recommendations for compensation. Sales commissions were the sole focus of the study.

I was one of the people selected to interview with the consultant assigned to study our branch. During our meeting the nature of her questions and attitude made it clear that her conclusions were preconceived: we were overpaid. She was only gathering evidence to support her case. When I pointed this out, she admitted it by arguing that we had been compensated too highly since the beginning!

Worse still, the affair turned out to be a double-edged sword. The diminutive executive behind the ruse was planning to use it in a run at the VP of Marketing in the home office. We liked this guy; he respected sales reps and was right hand man to The Boss.

We had given long months of intense days for over a year to build something out of nothing. My territory went from zero dollars to over $2,000,000 of production that first year alone. Now that we were realizing a respectable income based on results, some corporate climbing nay-sayer in his ivory tower was trying to take it away, mostly to gratify his ego. I was damned if I'd let it happen without taking my best shot.

I skipped over four levels of management and mailed a handwritten letter straight to our advocate VP. It turned out that the seditious study was news not only to him, but to everyone else including The Boss. Nobody in the home office was aware of the Napoleonic nerd's use of company funds to employ the agency. Imagine his surprise when our advocate tossed my letter on the little man's desk . . . after he copied it to the president, The Boss.

A couple days after the letter exploded in the home office Roy the Boy tried to muster a serious look as he called me into his office. He informed me that he had been ordered down through three levels of management to chew me out and that this was my tongue lashing.

We both knew that what I had done was against the normal chain of command but we also knew no manager could have done it because the message would never had made it to the top after being filtered by so many layers of executive fat. This is exactly why IBM has had an open door policy to the CEO making it possible for any employee to write a letter directly to that office and know it will be read. I had shot from the hip and the bullet hit home. Roy's serious face was merely minor theater staged for the other managers. We shared drinks and laughs and that was that.

Roy the Boy went on to become Southwest Regional Manager; he built our branch of the company into one that produced enormous revenues. How enormous? Enough to single-handedly keep the expanding national corporation branches from going bankrupt on three separate occasions. During the next three years he exploded the annual net profits of our branch from the paltry $200,000 it made before he took over to $1,800,000 his first year, $3,500,000 his second, and $5,000,000 his third. On his birthday, the day his three-year contract expired, the H.O.E.'s swooped in unannounced and fired him. Their reasoning?

1) He had done the hard work of achieving profitability and building the flagship branch of the company.
2) Now any puppet could maintain it.
3) They could save hundreds of thousands of dollars in compensation wages by getting rid of him.
4) They wouldn't have to endure him beating them up anymore over inane stunts they tried to pull on the sales force. If you're currently in, or heading toward a similar situation, get ready. It's not that it could happen to you; it will.

They added insult to injury by importing a Management Flunkee to take Roy's place. This guy's branch had never produced one year of profitability but they put him in charge of ours, the flagship branch of the entire company.

The first thing the Flunkee did was call a meeting to intimidate us into signing non-compete clauses. These are not recognized by Texas courts, by the way. We did so calmly and handed them in without comment. He smiled as he collected them, then left. Apparently the signatures of Lassie, Bullwinkle Moose, Theodore Roosevelt and a few others went unnoticed until much later.

HOUSE OF CARDS

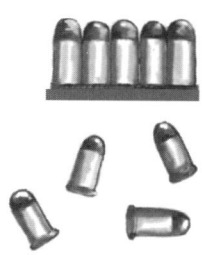

*I*t *only took Roy the Boy ninety days* to strike back. He secured several million dollars in venture capital backing, leased a new 65,000 square foot building and most importantly, signed a two year contract with the company's major base client that spent well over $2,000,000 a year in the program and provided the advertising vehicle that carried all the other ads market-wide.

Roy offered me a position as partner and VP in the new company. Despite my loyalty to Roy and the start-up opportunity at hand, leaving my $200,000/year job was not an easy decision. For years afterward I ran into people who stayed at the old company who told me that nobody could figure out why I left. Then they always asked me again just to find out for themselves. I could have told them it was because they fired Roy. I could have told them it was a matter of loyalty. They would not have understood; so instead I quoted Mike Hammer in *I, The Jury*. "It was easy," I said.

When I left, the top seven other reps joined us in the industry's forthcoming donnybrook. Our building wasn't ready for several months, so we worked out of makeshift facilities. We came in with the sunrise and stayed after dark; in the summertime those are long days. Sales immediately exploded because the old company had become complacent and arrogant as the only game in town. Clients enthusiastically supported our enterprise with scores of long-term contracts and we reached annualized revenues of over $12,000,000 in ten months time. At that point we were far ahead of schedule in retiring our venture capitalists' loan.

That's When They Sold Us Out

I came back from a successful call on a nationwide auto parts chain with one of our newer reps and found the offices in turmoil. Mo Fo Bro whisked me out a side door and said Roy needed to see me at a local restaurant, poste haste. Fuzzy yellow dice bounced on the string that suspended them around the mirror of my ostentatious yellow Ferrari as I crashed through the gears to our favorite Mexican restaurant. I jumped out and strode between closely placed tables to where Roy sat alone and quietly tasted his chips and salsa. "Well," he asked. "Have you been fired yet?" I replied in the negative. "Well, go on back. You're gonna be."

While I was out selling I missed the surprise meeting called by one of the vulture capitalists. He herded all front-office personnel into our conference room and fired them. They were told to pack their belongings and exit only via the front door. There, armed security guards frisked them and searched their briefcases before they were allowed to leave.

They Breached Our North Wall

During this chaos, executives from our former company arrived, their painted-tan faces beaming with smug confidence. One of my best friends called the biggest one of the invading group outside to the parking lot. Bubba kicked off his shoes and tried to engage the bewildered enemy in a fight. To his credit, the guy declined and went inside. Bubba would have kicked his ass.

The whole affair was a nightmare. I was thirty-two; all I had known in life was upward success. The sudden crashing defeat reminded me of my feelings the year before when I participated in the sesquicentennial reenactment of the fall of the Alamo.

A hundred eighty-six of us met in Brackettville, Texas on the set where John Wayne's movie was filmed. I was assigned to Crockett's group back by the doors of the chapel. I remembered the resonance of cannon blasts in my stomach, the frightening sight of hundreds of uniformed Mexicans storming the battlements. The cannon blasts shocked my ears. My mouth was as dry as the southwest Texas dust that blew up in the March gusts of wind.

It took forever to load a muzzle-loader after a shot. Suddenly a horde breached the north wall and flooded through into the grounds. I saw guys I knew bayoneted. Several around me fell to volleys of gunfire. And there I stood, trying to reload my Hawkens flintlock pistol.

The soldiers ran across before me in a file. I looked around and saw I was the only one left standing. They kneeled on command and aimed. I raised the flintlock pistol and fired at their officer. That was it; only one shot. Damn. I'll never forget what it looked like to see two dozen long rifles blast smoke and fire at me from a line of kneeling men only fifteen yards away.

I re-entered the present from this reflection and found myself standing atop our sweeping curved stairway that led up to our offices from the lobby. The onslaught was subsiding. By midnight the entire building was searched, ransacked, and all machines dismantled and removed. How did this happen?

The only person in our company whom we had not known personally for years was a financial officer. This genus Mustela mammal was put into position by the vulture capitalists. Because this guy is the kind of weasel who has no honor and would sue against a story that is the truth, let's say he did us no favors with our vulture backers, and provided them with a nifty little back door, just in case things didn't work out. Even though we were ahead of schedule and poised for large long term profits, our lenders saw the opportunity to make a quick killing and took it, killing us, too.

The vulture capitalists won; they made $4,000,000 over their initial investment in ten months' time. Our former company won; they eliminated competition that came within weeks of closing them out of the market. It cost the old company millions, six all told, not counting additional millions in revenue losses over those ten months. But, like the Magnificent Seven, we lost. 120 people were out of jobs.

The next night I drove home and slowed my wife's Mercedes 380SL to a crawl so I could savor what Joe had foreseen that day he called me into his office. He had told me that by the time I was thirty I would be illegal. He was right, and as I approached, the scene that spread before me was evidence. Our lifestyle resembled that of a bootlegger in a novel by F. Scott Fitzgerald.

Our half-mile driveway passed through custom wrought iron gates and wound through our estate across seventy acres covered with show-champion Texas Longhorn cattle. My beautiful intelligent wife had found and financed the place, a precise replica of the original King Ranch mansion known as Aqua Dulce. White ante-bellum architecture rose three stories above native grasses and culminated in a red roof that shaded two levels of verandahs, each of which wrapped around three sides of the house. The four-car garage contained our new Chevy crew-cab dually ranch truck, the yellow Ferrari, the black 380 SL, and a Toyota we used for a backup car.

In the eighties when Madonna sang, "Material Girl" it paid to be in debt and we paid ourselves well. Back then we legally deducted all forms of interest: home mortgage, multiple rental properties, car payments, credit cards, loans, and more. Cattle gave an agricultural tax deduction on the land, and we were allowed to deduct 100% of the purchase price of unborn embryos. We earned a lot, kept a lot, and threw ranch parties each autumn like those of a southern Jay Gatsby.

We kiddingly referred to the ranch as Tara because of its southern architecture. It had been a house of cards, and now it really was gone with the wind. It took years of work to gain, but only thirty days to lose my wife of fourteen years, the ranch, cattle, horses, cars, trucks, rental properties, credit ratings and the pack of wolves sired by Kimo and CJ that served as guard dogs in our three-acre yard. Maybe our lives were lived in a house of cards; maybe $14,000/month personal overhead was a bit high for a thirty-year old salesman . . . So?

Would I take same risks again to go with a Roy or a Joe? You bet your life. A deal is a deal; it should be honored. A colleague in whom you believe is someone for whom you go to the wall. Loyalty is the most important ingredient in a cooperative working condition, and

---

Integrity is doing what you say you'll do, not doing what you say you won't do.

—*Law of The Hired Gun*

Integrity is easy to have when everything is going well. When times are good and the coffers are full of coins, there's nothing at risk; anybody can stand steadfast with their code. But change the setting to one of adversity, put up something of value—the more the better—and only true integrity becomes manifest.

It's called putting your money where your mouth is; and sometimes you lose. Losing doesn't come easy when you've won all your life. The unexpected departure of your most valued lifelong partner at the time of greatest need makes it more difficult still.

Half a year after the divorce was final I asked my ex-wife why she left, if it was something I had done so I'd know not to repeat the error in the future with someone else. I told her it was OK to tell me whatever it was, it had been six months; it couldn't hurt anymore. She said it was only because she had changed . . . I don't think it was the loss of the money, we grew up together—married since age twenty—on not much money. I don't think it was the loss of our house or cars or any of the other material things. We'd been through tougher things and always came out stronger. I prefer to believe these were coincidences of timing. If she doesn't know and I don't either, who does? I was crushed. The only thing that pulled me through was that inner confidence instilled by my parents and by Joe.

I learned from this great crash: the most important thing is not why it happened, or how, or with whom; the most important thing about adversity is how you deal with it.

What are you going to do about it . . .

The reason wolves howl is to find each other when separated, and I was out there at the ranch on moonless nights howling with Kimo and CJ, hoping she would hear and come home, hoping to relieve the pain. But I still had a walnut plaque she painted for me when we were young and I put it on my bedside table by a window that overlooked hundreds of acres of native grasslands covered with beautiful Texas Longhorns. It was a quote from Hemmingway's *The Old Man and The Sea*:

"A MAN CAN BE DESTROYED, BUT HE CANNOT BE DEFEATED."

It's not possessions that are important; it's you. Possessions can be replaced. A strong self-image combined with successful selling skills will get it all back. What's important is the soul you see in the eyes that stare back from your mirror in the morning. Your personal value is not determined by your job; it's the other way around! The better you feel about yourself as a human being, the more you give of yourself into the things you do—like your job, your relationships, your income. It's the Law of Reciprocity:

> ## You get what you give in life. The more you give, the more you get in return.
> —*Law of The Hired Gun*

SO WHAT HAVE YOU DONE FOR ME, LATELY?

After the direct mail debacle I dived into a sea of telemarketing booths. (or "boofs," as we called them) In this tough environment the title to this chapter was a regularly used tongue-in-cheek expression, but its meaning was clearly serious. Here you were only as good as your last deal.

Upon arrival we were given a cubicle, a telephone, a computer and a territory that encompassed several states. That was it; no time for training; sales production was needed immediately. Minimum acceptable daily behavior was three hours of telephone talk time, over sixty-five dials-out and eight information packets sent. This was monitored in every division by daily computer printouts. The printouts were sent around desk to desk the following day, and your were required to initial your particular numbers. In this fishbowl your personal life was irrelevant, but your time on the job was managed via microscope.

The only goals we had were either for a month, a week or a day. The compensation plan changed almost monthly, but usually for the better—it always rewarded high achievers. The more we sold, the higher percentage we were paid, and in addition, if we hit certain revenue objectives we were bonused anywhere from $1,000 to $5,000 for that month.

Will Work For Spiffs!

On top of this, sales production was ratcheted frequently with spiffs if deals were closed on any given day. Spiffs were dead presidents handed to us on the sales floor, independent of commissions and paychecks. Spiffs ranged from $25 to $500 per deal and they made us feel like rich gangsters. On several individual days I made $2,500 in spiff money alone; my year-end pay stubs itemized enough spiff money to pay cash for a new BMW. We loved spiffs. Spiffs did not bring in more deals, but they brought deals in faster, and they lined the pockets of sales reps who were short on funds with much-needed cash on an instantaneous basis.

Everything was designed to manipulate the sales force into higher production each month. To keep us hopping, territories and compensation plans were changed arbitrarily, sometimes monthly. The pressure was intense; a lot of guys burned out. But hell, we didn't mind. We could light our cigars with C-notes.

Sometimes reps only lasted a day, sometimes two weeks. Sometimes they'd be there a few months, hit one big month of revenue and, like a supernova, burn bright and gloriously, then vanish. Six months later they'd be back telling tales of what a rough world it was on the outside. (No spiffs . . .)

I smelled the scent of big money, devoted twelve-hour days, nights and weekends, and within a year consistently earned the income I was used to making in my previous life. Apparently my philosophy matched the company's because despite the fact that the average term for a sales rep was about eight months—I was there five years.

Ranch Management

If you were excellent, you were revered. Less than excellent, you were gone. One of our managers came from a family that raised cattle; consequently he worked the sales force like he was continually culling a herd. Each month he fired off the weakest ones and replaced them with new recruits he hoped would be even better than his current top producers. With this method eventually the best become the worst. A rep could close three deals one day and be a hero, but if it went too long before their next deal they could anticipate a meeting in the Wolfman's Boof o' Death in which he basically asked, "So what have you done for me, lately?"

Manager: How many deals do you think you'll get this month?

SalesRep: I feel pretty good. I have a lot on my Hot List; should be good for at least ten.

Manager: OK, then we can agree that by the fifteenth you should have half of that, right?

SalesRep: Well, I guess that makes sense.

Manager: OK, we'll agree that if you have five deals by the fifteenth you'll be on track to keep your job. But if you don't, there are ten guys waiting in line for your booth. Five deals by the fifteenth.

For various reasons we became known as a bunch of Bulldogs. Each time a new rep made their first sale they were sworn into this bulldog squad with an oath and given their irrevocable bulldog nickname: Cy, Lazarus, Sneezy, SuperFly, Opie, MoFoBro, Catfish, Bubba, Vidale Sassoon, Cab Calloway, Bull, Deal Dude, Hosshide Jones, Buzzard, Bull, Mickey Mud Turtle, Dances With Skunks, and many more. (I won't bore you with mine.) At first it seemed we did it just for fun, but it was really subconscious psychological protection against the constant attrition of comrades in sales. If they didn't have real names, we didn't lose a real human being when they suddenly disappeared. Whenever someone left or got fired, we added their persona to the Graveyard, a cartoon of appropriately characterized head-stones on a hill bearing the name of the deceased rep.

Theory X

In "The Human Side of Enterprise," the late Dr. Douglas McGregor identified Theory X management as "the traditional view of direction and control." The notion is that human tendency is to avoid work; therefore people must be coerced, controlled and threatened with punishment in order to produce. Theory X is akin to fear motivation and as old as Machiavelli. It can produce dramatic results in the short term, but cracks and falls apart under the weight of time.

In this setting of samurai salesmen, today was everything, tomorrow, nothing. Our manager made strident bottom line gains with his turnover factory. Then he decided to climb the corporate ladder.

He created a new position for himself as VP of Sales and bequeathed his job as national sales manager to me. The sales team I was fortunate to inherit was recruited and forged together through intense trials by fire. After six months of performing as if to the beat of some drum in a Roman warship, they only needed to be respected and guided.

I made sure they understood this was a different regime. I respected them as professionals. I'd go to the wall for them if they'd go through the roof with production. They fed off that positive energy like a turbocharger on a powerful engine and we did great things as a team. Everybody arrived at 7:30 A.M., and many nights I'd look out of my office and see many of them still on the phones at 8:30 P.M.

The most remarkable result occurred at the end of a month during which we fell far behind our normal pace of production. To rev our engines I started each morning with climactic boxing scenes from the *Rocky* series of movies. The last day of the month we cheered The *Black Stallion*'s come-from-behind victory in the movie of the same name. The effects on the sales force were tremendous. When we left those early morning sessions they were ready to chew on barbed wire and eat cactus. We finished the month with the second highest number of deals in the history of the company.

I Get Asked to Leave Town

My predecessor had averaged 137 deals per month during his six month tenure; my crew averaged 148 per month over the same span of time. Obviously production under my command was more than adequate. Nevertheless, at 7:30 the morning of my birthday, the VP waited for me in my office like the specter of Death. "We've decided to make a management change," he said. Apparently my Theory Y techniques bothered the CFO/COO types. Too close to the troops. I was outta there like a fat man stealing home in the World Series. But I could pick my division to sell in.

My staff didn't allow me to clean out my office. I was required to sit in my new boof in the new division while they silently delivered the boxes of my eccentric paraphernalia. It was one of the most rewarding experiences of my professional life. That division never saw the other side of 100 deals in a month again.

Plutarch wrote that the measure of a man is how he bears up under misfortune; for me, it was time once again to make lemons into lemonade. The division I moved to was brand new. Previously, the biggest deals in the company sold for about $6,000 each. In my new division the deals averaged $10,000 to $35,000, two to six times as much. The execs were nervous about production as none had begun to take shape, so they created an all-star sales team. They pulled together the #1 reps from each of the different divisions and created one super sales team. Hell, I was honored to be part of it. Something about this particular deal jelled with me, and I became the #1 salesperson not only of this all-star group but over the entire company of over 300 reps, and stayed that way for four years in a row.

Meanwhile, turnover ran rampant among management ranks. The VP who promoted and whacked me got whacked himself and was replaced by a kinder gentler executive, under whom I was #1 again. After eighteen months, this guy mounted up and rode out. I had always respected his integrity, so I drove to his house and asked why. He had glimpsed the future direction of the company and didn't like what he saw.

His replacement was a guy who had the right ideas, but the wrong tactics. He blew in with the subtlety of a Tasmanian Devil and gave himself the responsibility of straightening out every department in the company. I performed just as well under him, but the upper echelon cronies were nervous about this bull in their china closet. The first thing this guy did was whack our sales manager. Why? Our boss was too tall and too confident. Just one month earlier, our sales manager received two prestigious company awards at the annual ceremonies: Highest revenue among all divisions and biggest percentage increase in revenue over the previous year. That VP was also gone after eighteen months.

None of this bothered those of us in the trenches. We had been through three VP's with three styles of management. The sales structure had changed each time, but the Bulldogs performed well anyway. That is, until the...

Invasion of the Pinheads

In the next management shift (I'm so sick of trendy overused business hipster phrases like "paradigm shift") these fellows landed in waves and all looked the same: retro-fifties short-cropped hair, white oxford button-down shirts, spectacles and peach-fuzz faces that rarely felt the edge of a razor. They didn't speak in terms we knew and responded to, but in textbook geek-speak. They were appropriate for the next stage of the company's direction, but this direction was one for which we weren't prepared.

Results were no longer top priority; procedures and appearances were. Meanwhile, sales spiraled down like the losing fighter plane in a dog-fight. Whereas our one division had produced over $500,000 revenue per month for months in a row in the past, under these pinheads we were lucky to approach $200,000. It was obvious that priorities had changed, but it wasn't obvious why. In retrospect I disappoint myself. Any fool should have known the company was poised to be sold.

CAUGHT IN A CROSSFIRE

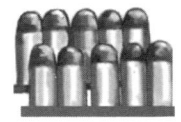

*(Following is my side of this fiasco.
There undoubtedly is another side—but mine's the one that's right.)*

> **The faster you increase your rate of speed, the greater your loss of peripheral vision.**
> —*Law of The Hired Gun*

This story of my firing from a $170,000 job is the narrative of a Hired Gun secure in his self-produced station, blazing headstrong and headlong into a firefight, trusting his support, and getting bushwhacked. Not unlike Marshal Duncan in *High Plains Drifter*, I found myself suddenly caught between three cravens with bullwhips and flogged to death as town leaders cowered in the shadows and withheld aid.

Keep in mind that at this particular company I produced a successful track record for five years: managed the top producing sales force, and received four awards as the #1 producing rep with production nearly twenty percent higher than the second-highest sales rep every year.

Why I Excelled

Often I was asked by management to speak to the sales force about how to be successful in their jobs. My principle message was a good old-fashioned iron-willed work ethic. I plainly stated that I knew and respected others who could close deals better. Also, there were others who made slicker presentations. But there wasn't anybody who worked harder or kept a fuller pipeline.

My day started at 6:30 A.M. I usually went home twelve hours later. I trusted my numbers more than my skill. If I had three times as many deals on my hot list as I needed to close, I believed the odds were in my favor. Usually, they were. The only other person who consistently kept the hours I did was the newest sales executive, Pinhead Rex. About twice a week he visited my boof before the sun came up and asked questions about how I worked my system. He congratulated me, praised me, told me I was "awesome." (That should have been my first clue; praise is one thing, but this bordered on hyperbole.)

Pinhead Rex must have obtained an MBA from the Slick Willy School of Decision Making. He came in from the outside, didn't know the business and neglected the advice of anybody with experience before he made ignorant and sweeping changes. Consequently, whenever he announced a decision we knew he would soon reverse himself with a "new direction" within a few days. These wavering leadership practices served only to undermine his respect by the troops. Indeed, he was a laughing stock of indecision among the top producers.

Lesson: Watch the Signs Around You

After a few months, it became common knowledge that Pinhead Rex lacked the respect of the troops. Therefore he was out to make an example of someone in order to assert his authority. He tried deft little runs at a couple of my colleagues, but abandoned them when they didn't hold water. As usual, I chose to ignore these petty politics. I had a job to do; I pursued it with my usual tunnel-vision focus and singleness of purpose. This is where I learned that my greatest asset was also my weakness.

Live By The Sword, Die By The Blade

My key strength in selling was this tunnel-vision focus; it was also my downfall at this job I enjoyed and in which I excelled. My undoing came in not observing the telltales of management. At the time, I was headlong in a rush to close eleven deals I had put into closing position and whose consummation promised handsome rewards. In sticking strictly to a sales regimen, I voluntarily ignored swirling political shenanigans. I had thrived through the years despite several complete changes in executive staff; games were their jobs, sales were mine.

This critical point in time involved the renewal of a contract with a state association that endorsed our products to its members. In this particular state the backing of the association created a tremendous advantage in sales. The decision makers were executives who had networked through the association for years. With the backing of the association we were in like Flynn, without it we were just another solicitous vendor.

My contact, VP of the state association, said everything on the renewed contracts was fine. Indeed, it was the same deal that we had the previous year. We offered a discounted rate to association members, the same as our company offered to other state associations and corporate groups. At the time, this VP was also absorbed in state politics involving literally billions of dollars, and suggested that, for convenience and time management we just use basically the same agreement and the same signature page from the previous year bearing his name and mine.

It sounded easy to me, but agreements of this sort required the signature of an executive (Allah) two levels above our manager. The moods of Allah toward sales were unpredictable, but our manager (Barney Fife) was pretty tight with him and worked on getting the renewed contract approved.

Each day I reminded Barney that the contract needed to be approved so we could bring in over $40,000 of new business that was waiting to close. He said he needed to wait until Allah was in the right mood. Finally, Barney said to go ahead and get the deals in; by the time they closed he would have the contract approved. Barney and I had performed this run-and-shoot offensive strategy several times before and everything always worked out fine. Ol' Barn wasn't the strongest manager, but he was good—I trusted him.

Allow me to interject that some entire divisions in the company were not producing $40,000 revenue in a month. Our compensation plan at the time paid $10,000 for over $30,000 in new revenue, and my eleven deals were on track to produce a total of $100,000—commissions totaling around $35,000.

Toward month's end both Barney and his direct superior were away for a week when five of my deals came in. I wanted to make sure these contracts were credited, so in their absence I took the first deal to Pinhead Rex, who initialed it. The subsequent four deals came in close to the time of the middle managers' return, so we put them on one of these manager's desk for approval.

Bushwhacked

I was on the phone to a client when this guy came screaming into my boof like a Banshee overdosed on Ex-Lax™ and made a violent spectacle of the deals and the association contract. This was very unlike his normal compsure. He accused me of signing company documents without approval, and of having his name on them as well. No phone call in private, no request for a meeting in his office, no civil demeanor or questions. Just a ranting tirade out on the open sales floor.

Unfortunately, his facts were correct. I had forgotten, but his signature was on the old contract, along with mine and the association VP, from a short two-month term the year before when we had no manager and he covered the position before they brought in Barney. I told him as calmly as I could that 1) Barney supported the deal with the association, 2) would be able to support it upon his return and 3) approval was already in process between Barney and Allah.

When the guy heard about Barney getting Allah's approval he looked like a cartoon character: his head spun, his eyes popped out, smoke blasted from his ears—sirens and whistles blew from his mouth.

(Oops. . .)

I finished the month with $100,000 revenue, more than most reps produced in a year. My reward was getting called into a meeting by Barney's boss and Pinhead Rex. Barney was conspicuously absent. They opened by informing me that Barney had a degree from the Ronald Reagan School of Amnesia; he disavowed any knowledge of the association contract. They then discussed possible punitive actions against me ranging from reduced commissions on all my deals (50% less), to termination.

I cited my track record: In five years with the company I had never had a single deal denied for any reason; never had one chargeback. I reminded them that Pinhead Rex had signed off on the first of the new association deals and that this was all due to an oversight on my part. I admitted it, then volunteered to take a polygraph test to bear out the truth of my claim that I only pursued this on the belief that these deals were legitimate. They ignored the polygraph suggestion, concluded the meeting. They'd let me know their decision.

Later the same day, Pinhead Rex called me into his office. I expected the Spanish Inquisition. Instead, he asked me to head up a Dream Team of top reps from each division to create another brand new division. Production in this new venture was far below projections and they wanted to jump-start it. I asked him to give me 24 hours to consider the offer and left, confused.

Let's see: in a morning meeting I was accused of lying, cheating and forging—threatened with severe punishment as an example to the rest of the sales force. In an afternoon meeting on the same day with the same executive I was told that I was a role model and leader that other salespeople looked up to and offered a high profile job change.

The next day I met with Pinhead Rex, said I appreciated the offer, but respectfully declined. (The income potential was half what I was making—see Chapter 14, "You're Not Being A Team Player.") I then asked him if they had reached a decision on my situation. He stammered in his usual fashion, looked around as if searching for a way out of a boxing ring, then said they were determining the level of punishment ranging from elimination of all commissions on the deals to termination.

With the triple threat of Barney's acute amnesia, the inquisition, and the Pinhead's golden opportunity to make the Ultimate Example by firing the top-rated sales rep, I didn't need the Psychic Hotline to tell me what was in store.

I immediately took the elevator upstairs and was welcomed with a broad smile by The Boss. He congratulated me on the great month and the $100,000 revenue. I thanked him, then cited the situation I was in. He looked straight at me and asked three questions:

1) Were any of the five new association clients upset about the arrangement stated in the association's endorsement? (No, they loved the deal; that's why they signed up.)

2) Was the association upset about the five deals? (No, they openly endorsed our products to their members.)

3) Were the deals good deals? (Yes, we had offered the exact same discount to the association's members the year before, and were currently offering the same discount program to other groups.)

As I left, he paced his office like a caged tiger and said,

"I better get on this right away."

The next day I ran into his personal secretary at the elevator. She laughed as she said, "(The Boss) had me go right down to the floor and tell (Pinhead Rex) he wanted to see him in his office immediately. That always shakes them up. They were in there one and a half hours."

Twenty four hours later I stared across the glossy veneered desk at our company's version of Dumb and Dumber. My look of disgust was reflected on the phony yuppified plate-glass spectacles of Pinhead Rex, who pulled me out of my boof for this surprise meeting.

> # Meetings are held for the benefit of the person who calls the meetings.
> —*Law of The Hired Gun*

He had been in his job a total of seven months; it showed. He continually averted his eyes so they avoided direct contact with mine. His stammering speech irritated me to no end. "Um, OK, unhm," he stated. "We have met and, um, it is, um, management's decision that in the future direction of the company, um, you are no longer part of that direction." Weak-Ass Corporate Geek-Speak for, "You're fired."

I was found guilty of signing company contracts without approval and fired. Of course, they accepted the $40,000 revenue from all five of the contracts. But I was paid none of the commissions due to me from those sales, a loss of $19,000 total income, including the $10,000 bonus due for total revenue achieved.

Smoking Gun

Prosecution, judge and jury were out. If the executioner had the decency to offer a last cigar, I would have had the indecency to puff a cumulous billow from a Romeo y Julieta into his face. His downturned gaze surveyed the top of the vacant desk, studied the bourgeois wall-to-wall carpet, and his hands fumbled to make a steepled posture. His thick-featured comical sidekick sat to my left.

The yes-man didn't speak, but that was no surprise. During his two-month career at the company his business vocabulary had been limited to one of two statements: "Management is taking that under consideration and we'll have a decision on it soon," or, "We're working on that now and we'll get back with you in a meeting." More Geek-Speak.

Consider the euphemisms he'd have invented if someone asked a *tough* question, like directions to the men's room.

Pinhead Rex was right. In the future downward spiral of this over-controlled environment I didn't fit. Nor did the Number Two rep a week later, and after him, Numbers Four and Six; then Number Eight. Cartoons circulated after each additional top rep was fired, captioned, "Silenced, because they sold too much." The time to mount up and ride off occurred when the Pinheads arrived en masse like so many carpetbaggers. When the leaders who shot straight in twenty-five words or less were gone and the graduates of Stupid School arrived, it was my fault for not getting out sooner.

I respected The Boss and didn't feel like whining to him about getting whacked. But I did want to know if he would be a positive business reference in my forthcoming job search. I called and asked. He said, "Absolutely, positively." Good enough for me.

It was common knowledge that The Boss had sold all his stock in the company; he was no longer officially in power. As long as The Boss was in charge you knew where you stood, and you knew it immediately. In the beginning, payoffs came in multiple C-note spiffs flashed into your hands ceremoniously before your peers the moment a contract came over the fax. The environment was new, intense, an excitement created by enthusiasm and esprit de corps.

**The deal is the deal.
Everything else is
just conversation.**
—*Law of The Hired Gun*

The Boss founded the company on a hunch and his own capital, hired the best guns in the business to get the job done. The company opened with one division, one idea. A year later it had two; two years later, four. The following year it went ballistic into eighteen divisions and was one of the top ten fastest growing companies in the United States. When we hit twenty-two divisions and hundreds of millions in stock value, The Boss sold as many shares as he was legally allowed, when the timing was best. Unfortunately for salespeople, this meant he basically scooped himself up out of the broth, and the beancounters at the bottom floated to the top. The beancounters made sure that the company's textbook managers looked the part of a *Wall Street Journal* ad and positioned the business for sale.

It took five years to build this palace of production. The crew was several hundred aggressive reps who competed with each other on a healthy basis from seven A.M. to six P.M. every day. By contrast, it only took five months of Pinhead Management to deteriorate the neighborhood to an unproductive slum. Then, if you took a walking tour at four o'clock any given afternoon you might find a dozen reps.

It came as no surprise when the company was sold a few months after my departure. I found it hilarious when The Boss opened another venture and hired away the same mercenaries of sales that had been with him from the beginning. Good for him and good for them. The Magnificent Seven saddled up and rode to one more town further west.

When executives feel inadequate because one or two sales reps take home bigger paychecks than they do they often seek to relieve this self-imposed stress by eliminating not the cause, but the symptom. The cause is their feeling of inadequacy. The symptom is their visualization of the rep as an enemy; one who earns a respectable income because of merit, because of measurable production, something they couldn't do.

If and when you determine that you have this kind of executive in power over your company or your division, it's time to consider moving on. Know when to hold 'em and know when to fold 'em. The insecure executive usually wins over the sales rep, just as the craven politician usually wins over the warrior. They have all day to plot and scheme. Meanwhile you're out focusing on production. It isn't a level playing field. These people will do whatever they can to trump up reasons to eliminate you so they can feel more secure about their tidy little positions.

Remember, the company offered you a position; you made the decision to take it. You owe the company your loyalty and very best efforts. Put the company first, until it puts you second. When you smell political sabotage remember also, you're the Hired Gun.

Epilogue

A couple years later after the new owners learned that procedures didn't pay the bills as well as sales, Pinhead Rex was whacked.

HAVE GUN, WILL TRAVEL

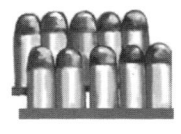

*T*he morning after my departure from this once-glorious company, my telephone rang at home. I was hoping to sleep past five A.M. for the first time in a year, but Roy the Boy's familiar voice woke me.

Since our initial days together in the direct mail business he had established his own successful mailing company in Tennessee. He said, "Flash, I need a Hired Gun. The manager in one of my branches tried to pull a power play and take over the business. I just fired her, two sales reps, and the secretary. I need to save that market. Are you available for the next couple weeks? All expenses, salary and commission."

I caught a plane to the Volunteer State that afternoon. It was snowing in Tennessee when we tried the cold steel lock on the door at Roy's branch office. The key worked, but that was all that did. The place was a shambles. When his manager left, she took the secretary and two reps with her, as well as a lot of files, file cabinets, the computer, and other miscellaneous equipment. It was Sunday, and there didn't seem to be a lot we could do, but I straightened out what was left of the office records and faxed invoices to every client who still owed money from the mailing that had just gone out.

The next day we were joined by another member of our direct mail days in Dallas and Roy's sales manager from another nearby market. We split into two teams and prioritized our activities:

1) Collect outstanding checks from clients who had just been mailed,

2) Reassure them that the company was in good shape and continued to function smoothly, despite some personnel changes,

3) Sign contracts and collect artwork for the next issue to be mailed,

4) Interview and hire two new sales reps with local print media experience.

It wasn't as easy as it sounds. The manager made her run at setting up her own business using Roy's clients. By the time we saw several of them in the course of our work, she had already been there spreading lies and innuendo.

By the time the dust settled two weeks later she had one client; we had all the rest. Unfortunately that client lost the prime position on the front cover of the publication they had enjoyed throughout the previous year. When they announced their allegiance to her we immediately sold it to someone else on a twelve month contract.

This may sound like our run at our company in Big D back in the old days, but the causal circumstances were entirely different. In our case, a boss who was loyal to the company was fired out of corporate greed. By contrast, this disloyal local manager didn't know anything about the business when she started. Roy gave her a job and taught her everything she knew. She was fired because she had already begun to set up her own operation after learning the business at Roy's expense.

When I left at the end of two weeks the ruckus was settled. All monies due were collected, the forthcoming issue was completely sold out and two new sales reps reported for their jobs at the refurbished office.

Peacemaker

When my return flight touched down in Dallas I drove to a business owned by a friend to surprise her and take her to lunch. She was the owner of an exciting new business with annual revenues in solid seven figures. When I arrived, I learned that she and her entire staff were already out, celebrating. I caught up to them at a restaurant and quickly deduced that this was actually a demonstration of a stiff upper lip by my friend. Unfortunately they had just lost their biggest client at the end of a turbulent speakerphone teleconference, to the tune of $2,000,000, that morning.

As we shared champagne it became obvious that creation of new revenue was suddenly a very high priority. I wasn't too busy at the time and volunteered to help bring in new business. The offer was accepted somewhat enthusiastically.

A week later on a Caribbean beach she said, "I'll pay you $10,000 if you get them (the large client) back." Ten grand isn't a lot of money to recapture a lost two million, but at the time I needed cash; I considered the sum a full three seconds and said, "OK." That afternoon I called the client's frozen offices in the Great White North from a chaise longue on the beach and introduced myself to the executive officer. I half expected to hear the phone hang up.

Instead, he was cordial and invited me to visit their facilities in an attempt to work things out. There seemed to be issues of communication and customer service involved, but the reasons we openly discussed were not nearly strong enough to jeopardize this volume of business to the point of complete termination. I detected a cause that went a lot deeper when he kept insisting that they were really an easy company to work with.

We returned to Texas and I spent the next couple weeks learning her business and the problems that occurred with this client. When I felt halfway competent, we timed my visit to the snowbound northeast to coincide with a regular meeting of the client's management staff. Upon my arrival at the client's offices I was astonished at my treatment.

Due to the vehemence of the breakup, I planned a long hard fight up Porkchop Hill. Nothing could have been more mistaken. I was given a tour, offered anything I could possibly need to make my visit productive, and invited to dinner that night after the meetings concluded.

I learned a lot at the meetings, mostly by listening and taking notes. It seemed that most of the tangible problems could be solved with an increase in sensitivity to the client's needs, and in the client's understanding of my friend's manufacturing and economy of scale. There were occasional disagreements about the relationship between the two companies, but nothing that could not be resolved.

The Plot Thins

I developed a keener insight to the root cause of the estrangement that night over dinner, but learned even more before a fireplace in the hotel lobby with a bottle of wine and several ladies from the company. The bottom line turned out to be a massive battle of egos between business owners. My friend can be as genteel as your matronly grandmother in a social setting, but smack a business plan in her hands and she's Godzilla in a string of pearls. Butt her head against the macho owner of the client company who chomps cigars and plows his Hummer to work through the snow, and you have a sequel to *King Kong versus Godzilla*. Tensions were relieved on both sides when it was formally made known that I was the designated full-time contact between the two companies.

Both companies needed each other. They were just being stubborn children—with $2,000,000 wholesale and about $6,000,000 retail in the balance. (And they say sales reps are immature!) Two months from the day I accepted the assignment we were shipping to stores nationwide once again. Peace was restored, and I added twenty independent stores to handle the line in addition.

Interestingly, as soon as cash flow was restored, her company had a new direction for additional revenue that didn't involve me. The new priority was introduction of a new line to be added by all existing stores— a brilliant marketing tactic and an immediate infusion of huge revenues—that did not require my services. The Hired Gun had done the job, but corporate needs had changed so it was time to ride on. We both knew it was a short term deal; parting was profitable for both of us and we're friends to this day. But the fate of the Hired Gun is consistent, even among bosom buddies.

PROFILE OF
THE HIRED GUN

*B*y this point you know you're a true mercenary of sales, but I've added this chapter for two reasons :

1) So aspiring sales reps with a sincere desire of getting to the top can see the direction in which they're headed, for better or for worse, and plan for it.
2) So MBA textbook managers can appreciate characteristics of the sales reps who make them look good, but whom they'd rather not have to manage. (Actually, if you have one of these textbook types in your midst and want to do them a favor, give them a copy of this book as an anonymous gift, like in the old TV commercials about giving a bottle of Scope to someone who has bad breath.)

Primary Lesson

> **Student to Master:** "I want to learn how to do the things you do."
> **Master to Student:** "If you want to do the things I do, you first have to be the kind of person I am. It's who you are that determines what you do."

This may sound like one of those *Kung Fu* conversations between Grasshopper and the old Shao Lin monk with mirrors for eyes, but I heard this conversation with my own ears after a professional development seminar. I'll qualify the fact that it was a couple of Americans speaking. It's a terrific lesson, and bore repeating here, but I qualify this because I'm tired of the late trendy posturing about superior Eastern systems of business management, especially since those alleged Eastern management systems that emphasize quality were born by Dr. Edward Demming, an American sent to Japan to help rebuild that country after we won World War II.

Though I maintain great respect for the teachings of the Orient, it's bothersome when anyone reads their own press to the extent that they actually believe it. In the 80's, so great was Japan's confidence and arrogance that T. Boone Pickens was booed off their floors by chants of "Remember Pearl Harbor" from shouting Japanese businessmen.

But look at the Japanese economy today.

They'll be back on top before long; Japan is one of the most industrious nations on earth. Hell, we're not scared; we're blowing away the ecnomic record books in the late 90's, but we had our Great Depression of the 30's, our recession in the 70's, our failed S & Ls in the 80's.

There are probably a couple hundred books that have been published over the past decade that extol the virtues of business management with analogies and allegories drawn from ancient Oriental strategies of war and martial arts—probably a hundred too many. I have my favorites, and they are listed in the last chapter with others of equal value. But enough already!

It seems that two eminent businessmen were taken hostage by Middle-East terrorists. One of the victims was Japanese, the other American. As negotiations began to deteriorate, the terrorist leader addressed the pair, informing them that they were about to die.

"I will permit one honor to each of you," he said. "Before I dispatch you from your wretched lives and send you to Allah, you may each speak as long as you must to make final declarations of your solemn beliefs."

Then, turning to the Japanese he asked, "And of what will you speak?" The Japanese businessman replied, "I will speak of the many ways Japanese business practices are superior to all others."

The terrorist then repeated his question to the American, who replied, "Please, kill me first, so I don't have to listen to any more examples of superior Japanese business practices."

High Risk, High Reward

Combat mercenaries (not unlike us combat metaphors) can earn quite a bit of money. The difference is they can also lose their lives, whereas we only lose our shirts. Though our risks are different, our potential rewards are close. Our cavalier lifestyles are closer still, stemming from the reality that for both of us, our relative tomorrows may end without warning.

For every veteran who survives the wars of sales to gain wealth and success, there are hundreds of Wanabees who perish. Too often this is not due to lack of skill in the field or desire to succeed, but to their inability to survive the appetite of the corporate beast. They focus completely on fighting the identified foe, the business world outside their company, but inexperience leaves them open to getting fragged by their own ranks.

True Story

The following is an eyewitness account of an event prior to the 1976 massacre of mercenaries in Angola in which British soldiers of fortune were involved against Soviet-advised and armed Cuban forces. I've taken the liberty of comparing this tragic occurrence to a current business setting. Though the actual incident sounds unbelievable, it is true; and the translation is all too familiar.

Fact: A survivor of the paramilitary engagement writes that had he known upon his briefing in London they were to be led by a failed British paratrooper who was both schizophrenic and homicidal, he never would have accepted the mission.

Translation: If the sales reps knew the newly hired VP was an idiot, they would have sent out resumès immediately.

Fact: Many of the mercenaries were young and inexperienced. One night during a patrol, a tenderfoot fired a rocket at what he thought was an opposing tank, blowing it off the road. Unfortunately, the vehicle was one of the Brits' own Land Rovers. Nobody was hurt, but the incident became fodder for the worldwide press.

Translation: An overzealous new rep in a sales team hastily recruited as a bunch of warm bodies wrote up some unapproved deals. Though no monetary damage was done, some letters were written complaining about buying a product or service, and not getting what was agreed to.

Fact: The insane Colonel lost control in front of the troops. He ranted and raved, shouted at everyone he saw.

Translation: The idiot VP lost control in front of the troops. He ranted and raved, shouted at everyone he saw.

Fact: The Colonel made the men of the platoon involved stand against a wall and strip to their underclothes. He then demanded to know who fired the rocket. When the tenderfoot confessed, the officer shot him in the leg, then the stomach, then the head, killing him.

Translation: The executive publicly humiliated the inexperienced rep, then fired him in front of his peers.

Learn to forgive yourself

We tend to forget embarrassing mistakes we've made in our careers because memory is a protective device. It shields us from yesterday's anguish by pushing it deep into our subconscious. If you think back you can probably find an incident in your career in which you really fouled up, not unlike the lad in this story.

If you sell from conviction, belief, passion, high energy and commitment you can be assured that you will make mistakes. Fast guns weren't always fast. They missed targets and went off half-cocked many times before they got their timing down. They got over it and perfected their draw and their instinct-based aim. You've done the same.

When we make mistakes we want to be forgiven. The single most important person from whom to get forgiveness is yourself. After you've forgiven yourself, then go deal with others who are important in the matter. When you're OK with yourself over the matter you can deal with anything management dishes out.

> ## As long as you know you will fail more often than you succeed, you will succeed.
> —*Joe Charbonneau*

Consider this: Babe Ruth struck out 1,330 times. Somehow we don't remember that statistic—mostly we remember the 714 home runs he hit.

High Profile

Hired Guns are pretty easy to recognize. Because success is often affected by first and lasting impressions, they invest heavily in wardrobes, high-end cars, homes with posh addresses. And just as James Bond has Q to keep him armed with the latest competitive edge in equipment, so these emissaries of commerce carry state-of-the-art paraphernalia. It used to be the slimmest calculators, now it's the most powerful, most compact laptop computers. Soon it will be voice-directed palmtops.

While it's true that all this is effective, it's also true that it's all superficial. The only reason such accouterments carry weight is because of the personal value of the person who sports them around. So let's work on strengthening what's important; your personal value. Rewrite your identity statement because, as Ernest Hemmingway said,

"WRITING IS REWRITING WHAT YOU'VE ALREADY REWRITTEN."

Yes, you will actually perform this most vital of tasks three times, but there is no better investment you can make in yourself than learning through writing exactly who you really are. So once again, ready? Let's go for it . . .

Identity Statement For: _____

_____
_____
_____
_____
_____
_____
_____
_____
_____
_____
_____
_____
_____
_____
_____
_____

MURDERER'S ROW—
INTERVIEWS WITH
#1 SALESPEOPLE

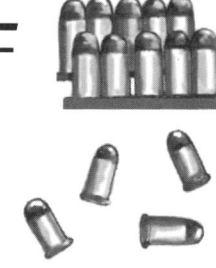

*T*he *1927 and 1961 New York Yankees* displayed such awe-some power at the plate that opposing pitchers dreaded facing them. Babe Ruth and Lou Gehrig, Roger Maris and Mickey Mantle; in each of these different baseball eras these sluggers were known as Murderer's Row. (The 1961 Yankees combined for 240 home runs in an era devoid of designated hitters.) This chapter is composed of interviews with a similar set of killer home run hitters, top producing salespeople.

The masters of sales you meet here are the kind the competition fears and respects, the kind rival companies wish weren't selling against them, and wish were selling for them. These sales reps live the life of the Hired Gun. You may not identify with all of them, but you will very likely identify with at least one of them. Their interviews reveal how they made it to the top, what happened when they got there and how they dealt with it. It illustrates why, in the end, one started her own successful business, why one left the field entirely, while another continues to battle management at his same company, and yet another moves from one company to another almost annually.

Their commerce is vastly different. It varies from print media advertising to educational television, from high-end printing equipment to computer technology. Their incomes are similar, in the top two percent income bracket among Americans. Their trade is the same—sales.

Susan

Susan: You know what, everyone told me I belonged in sales. I was going to college, waiting tables. And everyone said, "You should get in sales. You belong in sales."

Hired Gun: What did you take in school while you were waiting tables?

S: I was taking night classes in communications—but no real focus.

HG: That's interesting; another interview in this book, Tommy, and I both did the same thing. Communications.

HG: But I really had no clue what I wanted to do. I worked in downtown Chicago in my early twenties, partied, went to school. Partied—party, party, party. When I got out and needed to get a job I went for a sales job.

I got into a company that's no longer around—made friends with a woman who taught me everything. I got really into personal motivation, tapes—and she gave me the book, *The Magic Of Thinking Big*. I still have it at home; I even have the tape at home, too. And every once in awhile I still listen to it.

HG: What did it do for you?

S: It changed my whole thinking of life. Taught me how to see the big picture. Anyway, this first job was multi-level selling, you know, where you recruit people and they sell and you train them and get more people under you.

HG: What were you selling?

S: Custom art and decorating accessories for the home and office.

HG: Were you selling in the home or in the office selling?

S: In the office. The whole concept was the Avon, the Mary Kay, the party planning where you get people in your home and you sell these products. But I did not relate to that kind of sale. I went to corporations and cold-called and knocked on doors and did offices.

HG: What kind of products? What did they actually buy from you?

S: Pictures like that one over there in this restaurant, pillows, rugs. I was with them about two years and recruited like fifty people. But I wasn't a manager and you had to manage these people. I am not a manager, I'm a salesperson.

HG: Big difference between a manager and a leader.

S: I just wanted to sell and make money. That's been my motivation—money. After that I moved to Dallas because my mother lives here, and met and married my husband. We were just married when I started selling advertising in a local shopper.

HG: Which is where you and I met . . .

S: Right, in the Dallas office, which is no longer there. And I got a territory that was really terrible. I mean, everybody laughed and said, "What a joke!"

HG: How big was that territory? One or two zip codes?

S: At the time, it was West Plano when there was nothing out there, maybe some car dealerships, nothing. But I ran over twenty accounts; and at the time there was nobody in the company running twenty accounts—I mean, I just blew the doors off.

HG: How?

S: By always listening to my tapes, having a positive attitude, working from cold calls . . .

HG: What kind of tapes?

S: You name it! Anything you could think of in positive thinking. It could be somebody you've never heard of, or somebody really popular—Og Mandino, Stephen Covey, you name it, I've read it. Honest to God, I can honestly say that I probably have over a hundred books and tapes. I've been to Tony Robbins' two-week courses, Tom Hopkins, I've been to his week-course, "Sales Boot Camp," read his books.

HG: Was all this while you were at the shopper?

S: All of it. I was there four years. Back then I was making a lot of money for that place, something like $60,000 just in my crummy little territory. Then I went into national sales and I didn't like that because you were always fighting internally over accounts.

HG: With other sales reps? They didn't have assigned accounts?

S: No, that whole system was so screwed up. And then I decided I wanted to move onto bigger and better things, primarily because I didn't like the whole image of a shopper and direct mail. I was tired of the sleazy company I had to keep.

HG: In-company, or out-of-company?

S: Both. So I wanted to go into magazine sales because I loved magazines. I just made the conscious decision that this is where I want to be. So I went to the library and I went through every single magazine and tracked down every magazine that had a Dallas office. I found that there was one that kept coming up, a rep firm that was a division of the local city magazine.

HG: And others, like Houston's sister publication . . .

S: Right. They had lots of magazines. So I called them up and told them what I wanted to do and they said they didn't have any jobs, but I kept on them for a month. I put account lists together and said, "This is the business you're not getting." I did analyses on their magazines.

HG: How did you figure the business they were not getting?

S: Because I knew what the accounts were, given the PIB (Publisher's Information Bureau) of all the accounts in the territory, that these accounts should be in your magazines, and they—hired me. But they said, "We can't pay you anything, but you can work on straight commission." And I said, "Fine."

So, like a month into it, I sold a huge $500,000 account to Radio Shack and I went back to them with the order and I said, "OK, now you need to put me on a salary and commission." So I got on a compensation plan which really helped because right then things were really crashing in Texas and those were a tough couple of years. So six months into this job I realize I'm working my butt off, I'm making money, but everyone that worked in this environment was lazy, didn't show up 'til late . . .

HG: I remember, you really didn't like it after a pretty short time.

S: Well, the sales manager came in about ten, took a two-hour lunch, left at four. She was a joke. She was more interested in getting her nails done than she was interested in selling. And they had like, twenty magazines in this rep firm. The company ended up folding which is no surprise, they were so poorly run.

HG: What did you do then?

S: Before that happened, one of the publishers for this new magazine came in wanting to hire our firm. Believe it or not, everybody had plans and couldn't meet with this publisher, so they called me into the office and said, "Look, you need to go get this magazine for us." It was one of the top publishing companies in the U.S.

HG: Wait a minute; the publisher of one of the nation's largest magazines comes in and nobody can find the time to meet to take on a new book?

S: So they sent me—a sales rep. I just had a bad taste in my mouth; I thought, these people are sleazebags. And I thought at that moment, "I can do this on my own and make more money and do a better job for my people. I'll use this magazine that they won't even go see as my springboard."

HG: I assume your meeting went well?

S: I told them all about the rep firm and said that if they wanted the kind of coverage that they needed they weren't going to get it there because one person was working on eight books, someone else worked on ten books, they overloaded you and they didn't service you. So I suggested they may want to consider me doing this on my own.

HG: What was the publisher's response to that?

S: We hit it off really well. I said I wasn't in a position to do anything right at that moment because all of this had just occurred to me. I asked them to give me a week to put together a business plan. I sent it to them and a month later we were in business.

HG: What were you able to offer that the big rep firm couldn't offer?

S: I represented their book exclusively for six months and gave it the coverage it needed before I took on any other magazines. I told them they had to give me a retainer of several thousand a month plus commissions and they wouldn't be sorry. I went up to New York, signed the deal and started my rep firm with that one magazine.

HG: You started out alone in one little office space.

S: Then I shared space with a friend of mine who also had a rep firm and had an extra office.

HG: Meanwhile, back at the ranch . . .

S: Within a month, every magazine I worked on before called me and wanted me to rep their book. The problem was, I couldn't because I had made a commitment. (I wished I hadn't made it for six months but, you live and learn.)

HG: How long ago was all that?

S: Eight years. Now we have $6,000,000 in annual sales and represent eight magazines.

HG: But you really pared it back. I remember when you had twenty.

S: You know what it got to be? It came back to that thing where I don't want to be responsible for other people, and it was too much management. I did not like the management end of it.

HG: I remember at one point asking you about your decision to go out on your own and you said, "At some point I realized I'm not the kind of person who can take orders from anyone."

S: Yes. And that's how my husband came into the business. I've never been able to work for somebody I don't respect. Whenever that happened, I just left. Well, I had this one book, a guy's sports magazine, and to say I didn't get along with the sales manager is putting it very mildly. We just did not get along at all; it was plain we did not like each other.

He came to town to make sales calls and I was prepared to tell him over lunch, "I can't do this because I have no respect for you—" all the reasons why I wasn't going to rep his book anymore. But before I could, he starts with, "Look, I don't think this is going to work out with you and me, but I'm really interested in your husband."

HG: What did you think about that?

S: It really threw me for a loop. He had met my husband before, but he was totally into his real estate business. But he knew all about the business because he put the business plan together, did the books, the accounting and he knew all the clients because of the entertaining we did together with them.

HG: What did your husband have to say about it?

S: He's a big sports person—he loved the idea; which was good because it was a lot of revenue and income I really didn't want to lose. It was a great move because he attracted a bunch of other men's magazines to us.

HG: And now you've built this huge home on the country club golf course with your offices in a separate wing, you work together, play together. Wake up, you're at work; lock the door and leave it behind you . . .

S: The whole time with the company or anywhere I went I just have an unshakable confidence in myself that I can do anything. So if you have to say what's the secret? It's attitude—the inner belief that creates that attitude. It's certainly not skill, because it's not brains that make it.

HG: And for you this strong self belief manifested itself . . .

S: From *The Magic Of Thinking Big*. To me, this is just another step. I have a lot more things I want to do that'll make billions.

HG: Like in what kind of direction?

S: I have a lot of little ideas in my head. Any product or service for the aging population.

HG: The baby boomers—a wise man once told me that anything that appeals to that group will always make money, that the baby boom generation progresses through time like a big meal swallowed by a python—it's this huge bulge that goes on from year to year, like the big meal in the snake is this big bulge that slowly moves along until it's gone. And if you just figure what business to be in that appeals to that group at that point in it's age cycle, you'll do great.

S: I'd like to invent a product and market it to the public. Like Beanie Babies. You've seen those?

HG: Just recently.

S: You're not a parent. It's the hottest little toy out there. McDonald's just did a second Beanie Baby promotion. The first one was the most successful promotion in the history of McDonald's.

HG: So what's the deal?

S: It's a little stuffed baby animal that has beans in it. It's made by a company called Ty out of Chicago; they're sold out all over the country. I went to Chicago, went to every store possible looking for Beanie Babies—they're just sold out. Like the Tickle Me Elmo toy one Christmas. So something like that; I have these ideas in my head. But right now I need to be where I'm at. I work about thirty hours a week—at the office, work-work. I have incredible flexibility, make a lot of money. I'd be a fool to blow it off to start something new. At least until both kids are in school full time.

HG: So how long until we see the Tickle Me Susan out on the market?

S: About three and a half years. Then I'll be out of this.

HG: You'll be bored with building this and want to move on . . .

S: I'm actually bored with this already. I've been bored for about a year. But the money keeps me there.

HG: Your level of income buys a lot of boredom.

S: Yes; and right now my focus is more on the kids.

HG: So now you have how many people?

S: Five; we'll bring one more on in awhile—I'm grooming someone to phase me out. We built the house to have the offices as part of it so we could spend more time with the kids.

HG: And it all started with cold-calling door-to-door.

S: So many people do the books or tapes, but are afraid to actually get out there and do it, take action, make calls. I truly believe my experience calling on those little mom and pops door-to-door selling advertising was great experience. There's no better sales training.

HG: You know, almost every person I've interviewed started out in some fashion, door-to-door. Louis with vacuum cleaners, Steve with coupon books, I made my Christmas money as a kid going door-to-door shoveling driveways and sidewalks.

S: I think it's the best. Figure it out yourself. Get out there and do it.

Louis

Louis: I started off selling vacuum cleaners.

Hired Gun: Door-to-door?

L: Door-to-door. Are you familiar with the Rainbow?

HG: I am. I know people who still own some. They hold a reservoir of water that attracts the dust as you vacuum.

L: They still make 'em. I sold the Rainbows door-to-door, then I sold life insurance for Aetna. Then after that I sold printing presses, which is my longest term as a salesman.

HG: Web presses?

L: Some. I was doing quite well selling printing presses. The company I was working at was developing a new product, called the LAS—Liquid Application System.

HG: Around what year was this?

L: 1974. Nobody had ever sold an LAS; nobody had ever seen one. It went on the end of a supercalendar—a supercalendar goes at the end of a web to give it its finish. It also controls the moisture in the paper, which is important because that determines the quality of the paper coming off of the web. When you're making high quality paper, moisture is real important and you have to control it. They were having trouble controlling it and the webs would actually warp due to moisture. The LAS was able to minimize loss during paper production.

Well, my company was developing this new product. In the meantime I was doing quite well selling printing presses. They needed somebody to try and break this LAS out into the market. So they pulled me out of the sales area where I was doing so well, and they put me with the engineer who had developed the LAS to learn everything I could about it so I could sell this thing. They pretty much wrecked what I was doing selling printing presses, gave my territory to someone else because they wanted me to start peddling the Liquid Application Systems. But my revenue started dropping severely because I wasn't out selling.

HG: And why did they do that, do you think?

L: Because I was doing well selling printing presses and they figured if I was doing that well with those things I would do well peddling these new things. But I didn't want to give up my territory with the presses; I had a rapport with the people, I was doing well. There was no reason to move to the LAS at that time because they weren't ready to go into the market yet. But they put me with the engineer to learn what I could about it. So

I went in there and I learned everything I could about Liquid Application Systems.

HG: Then what happened?

L: The engineer and the company execs got into a tussle, so the engineer quit and took every thing he could find, engineering-wise to the Liquid Application System. So now, they've got an LAS sitting there. They don't know how to run it; they've got people coming up from one of the biggest paper mills in the country to look at it. So then they're all looking at me, like, can you sell this thing? I said, "Well, hell, I don't know." They said, can you run it, first of all—they didn't have anybody but me who knew how to run the thing to demonstrate it. Well, I saw the people from the paper mill, ran it, did a demo on it. Ended up selling *three* of them.

HG: That's impressive. They must have been happy with that. What kind of revenue did that generate?

L: At the time, the things were going for about $1.5 million apiece. Also at that time, when I was selling printing presses, I was on a seven percent commission. So I went home counting my commissions at about $315,000. I mean, I am feeling really froggy; I'm thinking, why do I need to work the rest of the year? I'm done. My year's made; I'm finished. I'll just lay back and go to the Caribbean.

HG: Somehow I get the feeling to say, "Oh no, buffalo-breath."

L: Well, I got this little bitty cheesy commission check. Freaked me out. I went to the head of the outfit to figure out what was going on. "Well, this product doesn't sell at the same rate of commission as the presses."

HG: You didn't know that going into the deal?

L: No. They told me, they led me to believe I should say, that nothing had changed. Their reasoning was "Well, because these are the first ones built, we can't pay that big a commission because of the R and D, the overhead—they gave me a whole song and dance. It didn't cut me down just a little bit. It cut me down hugely; I mean I got a commission check that grossed around $18,000.

HG: As sales commission on a deal worth $1,500,000.

L: Times three—$4,500,000! I mean, they chiseled it down to nothing. Then they said, "When you sell more, after these first three, we'll beef it back up again and everything will be cool."

So then I got pissed, and I said, "OK, look. You've already sold three of these things; I want to sell presses. That's what I was doing; that's what I'm good at. I've always made money for the company selling presses. Let me back out there in a good territory."

They didn't give me a good territory. They sent me to the worst territory. Everybody knew it was the worst territory. They gave me Missouri, Kansas and Nebraska.

HG: Dairyland. In the computer software business it's a joke. The reps in any company call that territory dairyland to be facetious.

L: People up there were still printing by etching things on rocks and slapping them together.

HG: Maybe they wanted you to develop a new territory.

L: Yeah, right. I'm up there busting my butt and I'm getting dirty letters from all these sales managers, "Why aren't we productive, why aren't we doing anything?" I mean, I was the top guy in the company before and was having a hard time of it there. Nobody could develop this. So what they did was, they laid me off while I was up there.

HG: Was this while you were up making sales calls?

L: No, worse. I had left Dallas. They had moved me up there to Missouri so I could travel these three states. This was in my second year up there. I had made some sales, but they weren't anything like the numbers I was producing before when I was in Texas. My numbers were considerably down, but I was developing the territory. I had made some sales, but it just wasn't what they were used to seeing from me. And they were really on me about it. They said, "But you've got three states . . ." And I said, "I've got three states of grass . . ." This was my second year up there and I had made some inroads. I was thinking I might make something out of this after all, and that's when they laid me off. And I'm up there in Missouri, and I can't get home. I'm laid off. I called them on the phone and said, "What's going on? I'm doing everything short of selling smoke and mirrors up here, I've finally got things starting to move, and you lay me off so I can't even get home?" Well, I made enough waves that they decided to at least move me back to Dallas.

HG: To sell here?

L: No, they moved me back to Dallas, but I was still laid off for a month. Actually, I wasn't. I was being punished for some reason, at least that's the way I felt, because I couldn't figure the thing out. And in the meantime they built the LAS's, and guess what happened? Somebody else wanted some of them.

HG: Don't tell me. They wanted you to go in and sell the LAS again.

L: Well, I'm laid off. I'm not there anymore. I had started my own office supply company out in the suburbs and was doing pretty well with it over a couple of years. Then I got a call and they wanted me to come in and talk to them. I didn't know who they were at first; I hadn't heard from them in a couple of years. Anyway, I went by to see what they wanted and I found out what the deal was. They had someone who wanted to buy one of the LAS's and they couldn't even figure out how to run the demo unit I had done for them before. So they said they wanted me to go back to work for them.

HG: And what did you say to them?

L: I said, "No, you don't. You just want me to come back to run these things so you can sell some more LAS's and then you're going to fire me again. That's how it was last time, so how do I know it's going to be any different this time?" So I offered to be an independent contractor to them. I said, "I'll tell you what I'll charge you to come in and run those machines for you."

I charged them $30,000 to run them for two weeks and I left. And I sold several more of them. Really, they got a great deal. Anyway, I went back to my office supply but that went down the tubes. I got married and brought my wife into it and that became a nightmare; we got divorced and I thought about selling it but I decided I don't want to sell anything else as long as I live. The Fire department was hiring, I knew there wasn't any money in it, but I thought, I'll just be a fireman and never have to worry about any of this again.

HG: So, you're saying you decided to get out of sales because of the stress and the pressure of being in sales . . .

L: Definitely—you can be doing well, which I was doing extremely well, and still get dumped on, extremely big. Like by flying elephants. Sales, I found, you do not have to do poorly to have problems with doing your job. In fact, I found out, people get jealous when—you see, I was getting bigger commission checks than a lot of other salesmen that had better territories. And it pissed them off, and then all the trouble starts to happen. They hate you because you're making more money than they are, then they start backbiting you and ragging you behind your back. They claim that you're cheating, you're lying, you're stealing, you're unethical—anything just to make a sale. And when it's over, you're hung out to dry.

HG: But they don't seem to have any problems booking the sale on those alleged lying, cheating, stealing unethical deals.

L: Oh, they booked every sale. And they came up with more whiny excuses not to pay me when I made the big sale.

HG: Now Louis, let me get one thing straight. You made the conscious decision to get out of sales and go into firefighting because of the stress and pressures of the job. But firefighting is not what many would consider a stress-free occupation. In fact, it's very dangerous. A recent study published by the National Institute for Occupational Safety and Health on the homicide rate per 100,000 workers places firefighters fifteenth among all professions.

L: Let me see that. Do you have it here?

HG: Sure. Here it is.

L: Yeah, but it puts sales managers seventh, and salespeople twelfth and thirteenth.

HG: But before you went into sales you were on a LRRP —

L: Long Range Reconnaissance Patrol.

HG: Right, in Viet 'Nam. What exactly is a Long Distance Reconnaissance Patrol?

L: It's the first patrol to go out and scout territory, enemy positions, and stuff like that.

HG: And you were the point man on that, weren't you?

L: When it came up in the rotation. We rotated the positions. Everybody had their turn up front.

HG: When were you there?

L: I went over there in 1967 and stayed through 1970.

HG: Two tours? How old were you when you went over?

L: Twenty.

HG: Tell me that's not a stressful position. Isn't the point man the one who always gets shot at first?

L: Well, I was real happy when we got hit that I wasn't walking first.

HG: What was your outfit?

L: I was in the 101st Airborne Division on my first tour and the 173rd Airborne Brigade on my second tour.

HG: So you did two tours, which means you volunteered to go back; and from that you went into the perilous position of selling printers.

L: Well, I guess the grass is always greener. In a pinch you'll do just about anything. My price has gone up though, if I ever get another call to run the Liquid Application Systems. You know what they did? They went broke. And that LAS they had was the only thing they had that could have saved them. Honest to God. That company's gone, wiped off the face of the map, and the LAS is the only product that could have kept that company alive today. If I had a bunch of LAS's in my back yard today, I could sell 'em. They were just too greedy. They should never have fired the engineer and they should have encouraged the salesman they designated to sell the things instead of screwing me out of the commissions I earned for selling their machines.

Steve

Steve: My friend, Mark and I were in college in Minnesota and we were working for this guy who ran a crew of college kids selling coupon books door-to-door. Dry cleaning coupon books. The owner of the company would go to a dry cleaner and say, look, I'm going to print up all these coupon books and I have these college kids who sell them door to door. You don't have to pay for printing, you don't have to do anything, except accept the coupons for discounts when the people come in, and sign here, right here.

What did the dry cleaners have to lose? Nothing. It was all extra business to them. Gravy. First of all, the cost of dry cleaning a shirt or suit is minimal compared to what they charge.

Anyway, we came to your house and I'd say, "I'm with Mayflower Dry Cleaners. Have you used us before? Do you know who we are?" Normally they'd say that no, they use one that's on their way to work every day. I'd say, "Great, well that's why I'm here. I'd like to try to get you to come down and try us out. I'm selling this coupon book for $9 and it's worth $50 in savings. Buy this book for nine bucks, come down and try us out." That's not exactly how the pitch went, but you get the idea. Six out of ten people would buy it.

Keep in mind the dry cleaners have no money going out, and the owner of our company has ten to fifteen kids going out every night of the week, Monday through Sunday. He paid us $3.00 per coupon book we sold if we sold under ten that night. When we were over ten books for the night, he paid us $3.50. When we got over fifteen books he paid us $4.00 a book. So we were making between eighty and a hundred bucks a night. On the other hand, the owner of the company was raking in over five or six hundred bucks a night.

HG: Also, as his volume went up, his margin went up.

S: Absolutely; it was unreal. Now, Mark and I were dumb, but we weren't that dumb. We said, why should we be doing this, slaving our asses away when he's sitting in his car smoking cigarettes while we're out selling door-to-door. So Mark and I put our heads together and said, let's go to Austin, Texas. We'll do this in Austin and finish our school.

HG: Why did you choose Austin?

S: The previous year we went on a spring break trip down to South Padre Island and we stopped in Austin for two nights and thought Austin was— Mecca. To this day I love Austin. Mark and I loaded up our van with our motorcycle. We only had one motorcycle between us. We had hair down to our butts; no lie. My dad basically said, "Good luck. Here's a thousand bucks to get you on your way. And that's the only money I had. Mark had a thousand bucks, too. We ended up in Dallas after driving all night drinking Bartles and Jaymes peach wine coolers.

We stayed in a cheap highway motel right across the street from Robert Tilton's Word of Faith Ministries. We pulled in at about nine o'clock in the morning and we slept for something like a day and a half. We got up that night to go out and find some girls and see what Dallas is all about— and we never left.

HG: Never made it to Austin.

S: Nope. Then we went out and in one day we contracted three dry cleaners.

HG: Still had the long hair and everything.

S: Still had the long hair down to my butt, I had an earring in, shorts down to my knees and high-tops. Mark and I were rugged sons-of-bitches. We walked straight into these places and we looked like guys who came straight from Jamaica or something. The first dry cleaner we contracted was in Mesquite, Texas and I'll never forget, the guy just looked straight at us and said, "You've got to be kidding me. You're not going to charge me anything, and you're going to print up all these coupon books and you're going to go sell them door-to-door and you're going to get me new customers in." We said, "Yeah." He said, "Well, how much do I get out of it?" We said, "Nothing. We keep everything we get. Everybody knows that in Dallas, Texas dry cleaners discount Big Time because they charge so much."

So now we're selling in this guy's area and meanwhile we're staying in this little motel that basically, this place is called, "You come on in, give us five bucks and we'll give you a room." That night we went out and started selling. We increased our price to twelve dollars a book. We went out and sold twenty books apiece, made something like $250 each.

HG: Nice change. How many coupons in a book?

S: There were about twenty coupons in a book ranging from $1.50 off an item, to 50% off. So we took our asses out of the No-Tell Motel and moved all the way up to a Holiday Inn. So to make a long story short, for six months we lived out of motels and sold coupon books and were making plenty o' dough and going to bars and strip joints dropping all our dough.

HG: Only six months? Sounds like you were doing pretty well. Why quit?

S: We didn't. I just remember six months because we went back to Minnesota three times in that first six months just to show everybody how well we were doing. Actually, six months turned into six years. We went to cleaners and made sure they signed a contract that they would accept our coupons, then we went to the printers, and here's where Mark came out shining.

We went to a franchise print shop and made friends with the guy there and got him into going out with us, partying, carousing, if he'd give us free printing. He gave us free printing for six years. Zero costs. No graphic costs, no print costs, no mailing or postage. All door-to-door selling. All money in our pockets. Cash or checks.

We got to the point where Mark and I would just want to go out and party. Actually at one point we had a crew of ten people working for us, college kids from SMU. We showed them where to go and how to do it and we were banging down tons of dough.

HG: When was this? When were the days when people still answered their doors?

S: They still do answer their doors. I'll tell you what, if I ever need to, I'll go back into this because I know I can do it.

HG: I'll bet you've seen a lot of wild things going to that many residential doors at night.

S: Let me tell you; I've got stories you wouldn't believe. Stories you wouldn't print—but one thing you never ever want to do as a door-to-door salesman is you never want to go in and have sex with somebody.

HG: Specifically, why?

S: Because—they could call rape in an instant. You can be invited in, "How about a drink," all that stuff; then before you know it you're some sleazy-ass guy who was banging on the door selling and you barged in and raped them. No way.

But there were a lot of fun times. Mark would be across the street and we'd yell at each other. "What do you want to do tonight?" "Let's go out and play some pool and drink some beer." "OK. Make sure you get cash from everybody instead of checks!"

HG: Sounds like corporate decision-making at it's best to me. Let's move on to where you and I were telemarketing together.

S: You got screwed; everybody gets screwed.

HG: Occupational hazard; more or less. When I went back to that Christmas party a year later they all came up to me gladhanding me and shaking my hand like they're my best friends. The same ones who maneuvered around and got me fired when a simple questioning procedure or reprimand would have sufficed. But that's just the way it is. We have three words for it.

S: "You Knew The Risks." That's the story of that place. It's a cultivating ground for salespeople to come and make a lot of money.

Just don't expect to stay alive very long. I will tell you one thing, though. Putting that place on your resume is good.

HG: It's good in that you show you worked in a shark tank for a period of time and can back it up with a W-2 that says $200,000. That's what is good. It shows a documented successful track record in a pressure cooker.

S: You know, you do so well, you become too successful, and you become a target.

HG: I knew the day I bought the Ferrari and drove it to work that my days were numbered.

S: That was your mistake. The COO was still driving a Chrysler station wagon. They hate that. They like to hear themselves say those things don't matter, that they're above that sort of thing. But the reality is, their wife's ugly, your girlfriend is pretty. They're driving a clapped-out family car, you're driving a Ferrari. You have a paycheck of $200,000 and they make less than a hundred. Of course they have a million in stock options and pension plans, country club memberships, but they don't look at that. They look at the paycheck.

HG: So why did you decide to quit a going thing selling your own coupon business door-to-door where you could get drunk all the time and sleep all day, to go work in the shark tank where they time your every call?

S: Well, rumor has it, I still can.

HG: Sell the coupons?

S: Get drunk all the time and sleep. Of course, the hours are a little different. I liked the scam.

HG: Tell us about the scam.

S: They had a better scam than I did. Had a $ sign for the "s" on the front of the word. Hell, you trained me.

HG: And Cy trained me.

S: And I trained Mo Fo Bro. And Bubba trained Vidalle.

HG: That's the thing about that place. The people flow through like a river,

S: But everything stays the same.

HG: How do you remember all that?

S: Vidalle was the one who fired me. I like him, though. I respect him. He was the best manager we had, by a longshot. We just didn't appreciate him.

HG: Until he got whacked by Bob the Bullfrog.

S: I'll tell you one thing; I always tell my dad this. That place is a learning experience for me. I'm learning how not to run a sales force, how not to run a company, how not to do things backwards. You know, for this interview, I wish we had the whole crew here. I wish we had Cy, SuperFly, Bull, Mo Fo . . .

HG: So why are you still there?

S: Because of the money.

HG: Golden handcuffs?

S: Getting out of there is a double-edged sword. The best thing about getting out is just that—you're out. The worst thing is losing the amount of money you make there.

Let me give you an example of how it's being run today. Keep in mind I've been there five years. Yesterday I went into my manager's office. I've been the top producer every month for over a year now.

HG: Which means you produce more revenue than anybody else in the whole company. How many people is that now?

S: In the whole company, about 250. So I get called into my manager's office yesterday and he hands me this sheet. I've got it with me in my pocket, here. Ye Olde "Employee Warning Record."

HG: I don't see your manager's name on here anywhere. But it does say, "Substandard Work."

S: You'll never see his name on something like this. He's chicken. He has his big brother sign everything. Admittedly, he's trying to do a good job in terms of operations, but he's still the sales manager as well. They have him doing all this immaterial corporate busywork, cross-referencing this or that, documenting why I'm not getting enough phone time. Meanwhile they want him to be an effective sales manager. You know him; you know he can't do both. Now, he has basically designated me to run my division as kind of a player/manager.

But let me preface this Warning here. They monitor our phone time by computer: number of calls each day, total talk time, average time per call to the tenth of a minute, for both long distance and local calls. This is circulated in a printed report every day, and you have to initial the report next to your name.

This is OK for the losers, the ones who don't produce any revenue and don't do the job in order to produce. But if you're a producer who brings in the most money every month they should look at the bottom line, not how many stinking dials you made.

HG: You'd like to think so.

S: So they pull me in and tell me my phone time is not good, number of dials is not good. I said, "Maybe not, but I'm producing. I'm selling more than everyone else in the division, combined." Then I said straight to them, "Let me ask you this, do you want somebody who comes in every day for six months, puts up lots of activity on the phone and sells only one deal in six months? (They know I mean a specific guy when I say this.) I mean we're talking about long distance phone bills for sixty calls and three hours a day of talk time over six months with only one deal to show for it—or then there's me. Thirty calls a day, one hour and fifteen minutes of time a day, and production four times higher than anyone else in the division. I'm asking you here, do you prefer the guy who doesn't produce and costs you money, as opposed to me, who does all this business?"

Do you know what their answer was? "Yes. We want that kind of person."

HG: Did the term "team player" come up anywhere in here?

S: Don't get me started. I said, "So let me ask you this, you're giving me this Employee Warning Record because I'm making the company too much while simultaneously saving the company money on cost of sales by being more effective with my use of resources. And they said, 'Yes.'"

HG: Who was "they?"

S: My manager and his manager.

HG: And these were the specific words of your questions and their answers?

S: Yes. See where it says, Employee's Remarks? I wrote in there, "Please keep in mind that while my manager is doing his other duties in terms of operations and computer bars and graphs, I am training employees in my division, I am running the division. Thank you."

HG: What do you think is their motivation for this?

S: They're looking to get me out.

HG: Why is that?

S: Three months ago, my manager's manager admitted that he hates sales reps making more money than he does. He told my manager, who told me.

HG: But that's hearsay.

S: Until he said the exact thing to me, face to face. He manages by intimidation. Listen to this. A couple months ago I had just produced over $45,000 revenue and I missed one day. The next day he pulled me into his office and told me, "Steve, quit. I want you to quit. Get the #&$* out of here. I want you to quit."

I said, "No. I'm not quitting. I just made $15,000."

He said, "I don't care. I want you to quit. You're a bad example for everybody."

I said, "How am I a bad example?"

He said, "You've got this sky booth back here," (the corner window boof where you used to work, Bob). And I said, "Then why don't you put me in the middle then, you sorry son-of-a-bitch."

Then he said, "You're walking on thin ice. I'm going to #&$*ing fire you right here."

And I said, "Go ahead. I'm not quitting." And he didn't fire me. And I believe to this day that he didn't because he would have gotten into big trouble. He wanted me to quit so bad—I made more money than he did, and that's taking into consideration he personally took a $5,000 commission out of my paycheck."

HG: How did he do that? Why?

S: Several salespeople had left or were fired. We had several territories open. I got my manager to approve this one deal that I had coming in from one of those open territories. He personally approved it. He said if it comes in, it's fine. It would be mine. I mean, I'd worked on it for months after the territory was open.

HG: From the manager's point of view, that could be poaching.

S: Not when there's nobody in that territory. And especially not when you have the manager's authorization to get that account.

HG: Maybe I should add another chapter, "Who Authorized You To Make This Money?"

S: It'll drive you nuts. So I get my manager's authorization on this deal. It's a big deal and will put me into a $5,000 bonus level of production. He says, "OK, Steve. Go ahead. No problem. Don't worry about it." He and I always had a relationship where we could do these deals.

HG: Right. So did I.

S: Yeah, Really. So a month and a half later I get the deal in. It pays me $5,000 in bonus money, payable right away. That was on a Friday. So I come back on Monday and he says he needs to see me. So I said, fine, no problem.

It got to Thursday before he actually got around to pulling me in because he was so afraid for four days to tell me. So he finally pulls me in and says, "Look, we're going to house this deal."

I said, "Wait a minute. You authorized this. You told me it was OK to work this. We have an agreement on this."

He says, "Yeah, I know. But I didn't mark it in the computer."

I said, "Whatever. That's your error, not mine. It shouldn't cost me $5,000. Look at all the comments I've made in my computer documenting my calls and working on this deal."

We're arguing in there and his manager walks in. He says, "What the #&$* are you doing bitching at him?"

I said, "What are you talking about? You guys owe me money. That was my account. That was my deal. He authorized it."

Then his boss says, "Hey! I think you're taking advantage of him!"

So I said, "Quit covering for him." And I walked out. To this day, I think that's why he has it in for me. His middle manager is so weak he causes this garbage to happen, then can't stand up and say what's right, then his manager has to cover for him. All the time. That's when he threw open the door and yelled, "You're walking on thin ice you son of a bitch!" and everybody on the floor was shuddering, "Whoa!" That was the day I almost got fired from that place for the second time.

You know, I really want to just go up to him and say, look, if you're so afraid of salespeople making more money than you, why don't you just go back into sales again and make money and be happy?

HG: Because his ego couldn't handle it. He's been in management so long he would view it as a demotion.

S: Exactly. Which is really dumb. My buddy Mark made $220,000 last year out of his territory. The whole thing is so dumb.

HG: So what is your take on this turbulent profession of ours?

S: I love it. If you can't take it, you need to do something else. Nothing else gives the money and freedom.

HG: What about the insecure, intimidating managers?

VP: Hey, you know what our slogan was: "We hate everybody but us. And some of us we don't even like."

Note: Ten days after this interview the manager's manager left the company. A year later, Steve quit of his own volition and started up his own deal.

Tommy

Tommy: I once came under attack from executive level management within my company because I was making more money than the CEO . . . We'd built a business from scratch that was doing over $100 million a year . . .

HG: Wait a minute. I'm old fashioned. Let's go back to the beginning.

T: Hey! What . . .

HG: Oh, don't mind Kuma. She gets jealous if she feels left out.

T: As long as she didn't get left out at dinner.

HG: No, she's fine. So your start . . .

T: Oh, man, it's been a helluva career.

HG: OK. What got you into sales?

T: I came right out of the School of Communications in college. I forget how it happened but I ended up interviewing at this mobile phone company because I was fascinated by the technology. I wanted to get a mobile phone until I found out it cost around two grand.

HG: I got a great deal on my first cellular car phone in 1985. Half-price. $1,900. Such a deal.

T: This was way before cellular.

HG: You mean a true mobile phone? Mobile operator? Ship to shore?

T: Exactly. Ship to shore basically still operates that way. Really, I was thinking, if I could get a job selling them, I could get myself a mobile phone. So I got hired as a salesman right out of college. I was probably twenty-two at the time, maybe not even that.

They didn't put me in mobile phones first; they put me in pagers. This was when pagers were the size of a small book and only doctors and fire chiefs carried them. I did so well in that, they put me into the mobile telephones. The only reason they did it was I was able to sell. I never trained or anything, just went out there and talked to people and one thing led to another. They gave me the leads so I didn't have to prospect, just sell.

They were switching their phone system technology so you didn't have to go through a mobile operator and you could dial direct. So guess what; the phone goes from $1,800 to $2,500 then $4,500 then to $5,500 for a telephone that was basically a small computer system that could talk to the computer system back at the base in order to dial the number for you.

The FCC issued two types of licenses: one to common carriers and one to the telephone company. The problem with the telephone company was that because they were a Public Utility, they had to sign up everybody and their brother. Their rates were cheap, like ten or twenty bucks a month for basic service, but you could never get through on the phone—during

L.A. rush hour? Forget it. 30,000 subscribers in Los Angeles limited to something like thirty channels the phone company had—figure through the math. So the common carriers made a killing; they charged high monthly rates and some even had an answering service attached to it. They confined their entire base of channels to a limited base of subscribers. So the ratio of getting through was a helluva lot better than the other option.

So I had this list of the top 500 business people, celebrities, corporations . . . everything, in California. I had their phone numbers and all their info because they were on account. I mean I called on major oil magnates, movie stars, musicians—you wouldn't believe the people that were my customers. And I'm about twenty-two years old. I mean, they didn't like me at first, but when I showed them how easy it was; they didn't have to bark at the operator, etc. I had major studios, I had the most incredible clients.

Then I started working with a partner company that had this thing called a briefcase phone. This was like cloak and dagger stuff. It had these lights on it that would scan and the antenna was in the lid. You'd be driving in the car and you'd be trying to scan to get a channel and the lid would fall down on your hand. People plugged them into their cigarette lighters and the thing would go flying off the seat and tear off the cigarette lighter plug. It was a real nightmare.

HG: How much did those sell for?

T: Oh, those were even more. They were like, six grand.

HG: Because they were compact.

T: Oh, yeah. Batteries. The batteries would get so hot they'd melt your seats. I had a guy with a convertible who left the thing on, the batteries arced and the thing welded itself shut!

After I converted the base of clients over, there was really no place for me to go so I looked to this one company I had always wanted to work for. They were the only ones I ever lost sales to. They were the best ones;

family owned—it was at about the dawn of cellular. So I joined them, but it was a real mom and pop show. I mean, I had been working for some really big companies before. Dad was the engineer, mom ran the front office and the shop, some other relative did the bookkeeping and was the receptionist, they had a couple kids who were the technicians who installed the phones.

And they hated salespeople. They didn't want to have any salespeople, thought they were all dishonest and cheats. The only reason I got in there was a mirror of the reason I knew about them. The only time they lost clients it was because they raved about me, and the only time I lost clients it was when they raved about them.

I was getting tired of working for the guy who was my boss. He thought he was Mr. Wheeler Dealer Entrepreneur in his Hawaiian shirts, flashing his gold Rolex watch and gold chains. He drove around in this God-awful demo vehicle that had seven mobile phones mounted in it.

HG: Did he look like a cockroach going down the road with all the antennae waving around?

T: He looked like a razorback! He was good, though. He'd bring the customer out, demo the phones, bring 'em around to the back, flip down the tailgate and sign them up on it. He had it down to a science. I can't even tell you what he did to hype up the guys in his boiler room who did his prospecting. He even started dating this woman who was the top rep for a big national competitor who made their own phones and had their own deals with the phone company. So she was still working for them, but his competitors were giving him leads because of side deals he was making.

HG: How did that work?

T: There was a waiting list for numbers. You could hardly get a number and he was getting all these cherry numbers that ended in, like, 1000. Then he'd charge the customer a fortune for one of these prestige phone numbers.

So I went to the little mom and pop company. It was prior to 1984 and the Olympics were coming to Los Angeles. The account that everybody wanted to get was one of the huge Hollywood studios. All their location trucks had mobile phones in them, all their executives had them. I had the account with my previous company because they were all signed up with a private carrier. Then I lost the account because they didn't want to go with the crummy phones we were selling, so they were starting to buy phones from other companies. So I worked my ass off and I finally got the account and I had such a rapport with the guy, he helped me out when I was in a jam.

HG: What was that?

T: I'm driving home from a date about four in the morning—I had a Z-28 back then with T-tops. I'm tired, tipsy, and I'm driving along highway 405 when I hear all this wind noise and before I know it one of my T-tops lifts off and shatters in a million pieces behind me on the highway. $800 down the tubes. I'm the only one out there at that hour so nobody gets hurt, but the next morning I have to go see my contact at this huge studio. Of course he needs a lift to one of the back lots to have me check out a malfunctioning unit. It's cold and starting to rain and he asks where my T-top is. So I tell him the story.

He laughs and says, "I've got a warehouse full of these things. We use this same car in some of our shows. Every time the director thinks he sees a scratch on one of them, I've got to buy a new one. I swear you'll never find a scratch on one of these, but I must have fifty of these things in a warehouse back here." So he gives me a perfectly good T-top.

HG: Better job benefits than an HMO. What'd you do after that?

T: The next deal was my biggest coup in the business. 1984, the Olympics were coming to Los Angeles. LA was the second city to go up cellular after they did the pilot in Chicago. They switched from two antennae to one because they got the technology down, but we started carrying this foreign-made phone which I wasn't sure about. I was really competitive with the big companies, like the ones with Official Olympic sponsorships because even my own old customers wound up moving over with them because of the big promotions. I got so pissed off I started calling on overseas companies. Remember, this is a bona-fide mom and pop shop and I'm calling overseas—but it was to prospects who didn't seem to care as much about who the Olympic sponsors were.

HG: How did that go over?

T: Well, I ended up with one of the largest foreign car manufacturers. They had put together a fleet of top-of-the-line cars which were already bound for the US on a freighter and they wanted these phones installed in them. Remember, this is a business where a two-phone sale was really good. A three-phone sale was unheard of.

HG: And how many were in this one deal?

T: About fifty.

HG: Fantastic! So you hit this major home run; what happened back at the shop?

T: First I had to deal with the overseas phone bill that came in. It was astronomical.

HG: Did it come in before the deal was closed?

T: Yes. I was working on straight commission, and that thing came in. They were ready to take it out of my paycheck. I said, "Look, we're not doing anything in this market right now. I have to go outside." Then the deal for almost fifty cars came in and they got even more furious at me. He said, "First of all, I can't even get fifty phones! Second, I've got a garage and one installer, and the Olympics are in less than a month! What are you doing to me here! You're going to put me under; I'm going to get sued!"

HG: You don't mean (heaven forbid) sales outstripped production.

T: I said, "No, I've got it all figured out." The cars were being delivered to a receiving area outside LA. They had parking garages, power, lighting, everything. I got them to hire a couple more installers and they just went from car to car with a cart and put the things in. It was the biggest sale ever in the history of the company. The guy left town to retire after that and turned the business over to his son.

HG: So what happened after that? Where did you go?

T: After my boss retired I would have been selling cell phones in a walk-in environment. Like going to a Sears or something to buy underwear. One day my old boss walked into my office and dropped these brochures on my desk.

He said that one of his clients had been a friend of his and he told him about me. He said, "I don't know if you know this, but they've broken up the phone company so it's not just AT&T anymore. Instead of selling $3,000 mobile phones you should go sell telephone systems for upwards of $200,000."

So I went over there, and that was my entry. All of a sudden I'm in the interconnect business. One thing led to another and I ended up working for one of the largest telephone interconnect companies in the nation at the time.

Also, at about that time I became even more interested in computers. I used to spend a lot of time at the mobile phone company trying to learn about their computer system. These things were all mainframes and mini-computers at the time.

I was there a few months when all of a sudden this large competitor moved into our market because they had just been unregulated. The baby Bells could go into any territory they wanted to in the non-regulated side of the business. So they started up their own independent interconnect company to go poaching into our territory.

In the space of one week they hired twenty-five of the top interconnect salespeople in the market. It happened so fast that even though I had only sold a few systems even my track record looked good. So I went over there with all of my buddies and they hired us all. They gave us base salaries and bonuses and by the end of the week we were at this luxurious resort for the big kickoff. You wouldn't believe this operation.

This was the time they started to run data through phone systems. So once again I learned everything I could about running data through telephone switches from this carrot-eating freak of an engineer. Before I knew it I was the resident expert in selling data through switches. They had a helluva time finding out how I was doing the things I was because nobody else could figure it out.

It became a real eye-opener for me because I ended up going abroad to Japan for a briefing where the entire sales process is different than it is here.

HG: For instance —

T: Well, here I was used to having my own demo facilities, my own showroom for my company, the whole nine-yards on site at my company's offices. In Japan they didn't have the real estate for this. The manufacturers bore that entire burden. They set up retail type operations. For example, when you set up a demo in Japan, you had to reserve demo time in this huge skyscraper downtown on prime real estate and lavish surroundings. It was like going into the Nordstroms of telecommunications. Everything was on display in these showrooms, from consumer products and alarm systems all the way up to supercomputers.

You booked your clients through, and you greeted them and you bowed, and the manufacturer did your demo for you. All you had to do was bring the client in. It was a whole different way of doing business. I'd never seen anything like it. It was a tremendous experience.

HG: Would you like another cigar?

T: Sure. From there I started networking with computer companies, because that's how I was driving my sales. I drove more data through their phone systems so they'd have to buy bigger computers. I was working with the biggest computer companies in the world.

I remember I had this sort of mentor at the time. He drove a Mercedes; I drove a Chevy. He had just closed a deal for all the computers his company did for a huge military complex.

HG: How long did the sales process for a deal that size take?

T: Years. Probably over two years. Proposal after proposal. RFP after RFP. So I got experience in the government Request For Proposal process.

Anyway, he came to me one day and said he'd just met with a bunch of guys who were putting phone systems together with PCs. So I started with that start-up company. I blew them away because they didn't even have a desk or phone for me. There was one phone line out into the hallway for me. I sat on a folding metal chair with my briefcase on my lap and my little 3 x 5 cards with SIC codes so I could make cold calls. Within the first week I had my first sale.

Of course, I was very passionate about the technology, so when the customers came in, I showed them everything they needed to know. I was only the fifth employee to join the company, and the second salesperson, and in a sales meeting I jumped up and started drawing the whole configuration on the board. The president and vice-president's jaws just dropped. They said, "What the hell is this? You're supposed to be a salesperson, not an engineer." After that it exploded. I became Regional Manager.

I ended up getting a major international account as a client and as a reward they sent me there to open up the first foreign office. I hired an engineer and staff and traveled for a year training about 200 of their salespeople. We had one of those little offices where you walk in and share a conference room with someone else. We cannibalized every spare part we had sent up there, and in my own office we only had three people, but we had the most advanced network setup that we had glued together from spare parts.

My senior management was livid. They just about fired me. They said, "Tommy, we think this is irresponsible; you used these spare parts and you slapped all this together. And you've got the most extravagant office, more than us." I remember I was taking the President and Vice-President back to the airport and they were complaining about all the expenses, reading me the riot act all the way.

At this time the account hadn't netted much because we were still in the training and the roll-out phase with one of our major distribution channels. I'll never forget, all this time the Vice President was sitting in the back seat flipping through a major news magazine while the President was yelling and cussing at me about how they're going to cut back on expenses and they were going to shut the whole thing down. I mean, he was absolutely furious at me.

Meanwhile I'm driving the car saying, "Yeah, yeah, yeah, BUT . . ." and I can't get a word in. Then I hear from the back seat, "HOLY $&*%!" He had opened the magazine up to a two-page full color ad for our product line.

HG: That you had placed?

T: No, that our reseller had placed as part of the roll-out.

HG: Did you know about it?

T: I didn't know about it at all. I had no clue that they were going to do this. I was this small cog in this huge initiative they had to get into the computer business. I mean, I knew they were going to do some advertising but I never dreamed it would be on this scale. I couldn't believe it. I never heard another word about it. Suddenly I was a big hero. They ordered hundreds of reprints of the thing. The execs all had the ad framed in their offices.

After that another company bought ours and I didn't like the way they did things, so I resigned. My distributors started to panic. My clients said, "Tommy, you can't leave. You've trained 200 of our people. We're rolling out this product; we need the help."

HG: Did you go or stay?

T: We ended up with an agreement where I became a consultant. I was supposed to stay there for one year and help them get into the business. It ended up to be almost ten years. At the end of that we were doing over $100 million in revenue. It was unbelievable. Then you know what they did? They shut the whole thing down.

HG: You're joking. After all that.

T: This is a copy of my $100,000 bonus check I got after several years of service.

HG: Looks like the real thing.

T: It's a color copy. Now if I can only figure out how to process it again . . . You know, they launched a tidal wave of political attacks on me because I made so much money. Even tried to discredit me. They created the compensation plan—I blew it out. Then they freaked when they realized how much money I was making on the comp plan that they created.

HG: So what are you doing now?

T: What an experience, though. I wouldn't have traded it for the world. I'm currently VP of a computer company that's doing some great things with networks and multimedia. Now I'm able to do everything I love— designing, creating, managing a team of engineers and creative people. I do sales, I do everything: sell the job, design the job, manage the creative, work with the engineering staff. I love it.

"YOU'RE NOT BEING
A TEAM PLAYER"

I *absolutely respect and admire* executives who promote from within, recognize available talent and pay the price to promote exceptional individuals in order to multiply their talents among the ranks. Unfortunately many companies and their executives are not this way.

So if you haven't heard this favorite management accusation yet, get ready. When you maintain the position of top producer, you earn an excellent income and enjoy the freedoms bought with your hard work. It isn't long before the guys and dolls in the back room figure you're making too much money and hatch a scheme to reduce your income, simultaneously corralling you into a position of high responsibility and little authority.

The scene usually opens with an invitation to a private meeting with an executive Vice-President. (Remember—Meetings are held for the benefit of the one calling the meeting.) The conversation between Vice-President and Hired Gun goes something like this:

VP: I wanted to talk with you because your high production and leadership have been evident for some time now.

HG: Thanks.

VP: You may have heard that we need a new sales manager for another division soon, and naturally we're looking for the best possible person to manage it.

HG: Mm-hmm.

VP: You have the knowledge of our business, you obviously know how to sell well, other reps look up to you . . . I've put the idea forward of you joining our management team and it's been received very well. What do you say? Are you interested?

HG: I'm honored that you've considered me for the position. What does it pay?

VP: Your reputation precedes you. (Pause) Well, it carries a comfortable salary base, and an override on sales made by your people. Plus the typical management expenses and some perqs.

HG: Sounds interesting; how much?

VP: Well, there's a lot more than money involved here. This is an opportunity to grow with the company. It's a position that can put you in position to go other places here, as well.

When you're being recruited for another job and they hesitate to discuss compensation, don't walk— RUN to the nearest exit.

—Law of The Hired Gun

HG: I'm sure it does, but my personal accountant (husband, wife, boyfriend, girlfriend, CPA, cougar, wolf, platypus) keeps a tight rein on my income and expenses. I'd like to get a clearer picture of the actual compensation.

VP: Well, the salary base is $40,000; the override is flexible, but it should add another $20,000 or so.

HG: So about $60,000 a year. Is that right?

VP: I suppose, but I don't want you to limit your focus to personal compensation. That's what has kept management from looking at you more seriously in the past. Remember, this is a management position. This sales mentality you've so keenly developed needs to stay with the ranks beneath you.

HG: The only problem I'm having here, and please don't take this the wrong way, but I've been in the neighborhood of $200,000 for the past four years. This would be a 60–70% decrease in income and carry with it a lot of responsibility I don't have now.

VP: I think you should consider the overall team a little more than just your own personal lifestyle.

HG: You know, when I was in Little League, we had a fourteen game schedule. I hit twenty-eight home runs each season for three years, batted over .780 every year, played every position on the field. I loved baseball. Every book I read during summer vacation was a baseball biography. I practiced in the snow in February and pitched in my basement when it got too dark outside. But my team lost almost every game and finished in the cellar every year. When my family moved, I realized I could be anybody I wanted because nobody in the new town knew me. I ran track instead— won lots of medals and championships, lost some, too. But if I won or if I lost, I knew who to blame and who to give credit. I learned a lot from that.

VP: You're not being a team player.

HG: Without meaning any disrespect, I have to say that when the bill collectors and banks call me for mortgage payments and car insurance, the team never shows up to pay them.

Whenever someone accuses you of not being a team player, they always want you to give something up but never offer anything of equal or greater value in return.

—Law of The Hired Gun

VP: I've really gone to bat for you on this. I hope you'll give it your serious consideration.

HG: I fully appreciate that this is a serious matter to consider. And as I said before, I'm honored that you brought me up. But I'd be losing twice as much as I'd be making, have income dependent upon production of people I didn't hire. I know these people, and some of them don't have the commitment I require. I'd spend most of my time in meetings, be responsible for reports and budgets, and be bound to an office all day. I like my freedom, I like sales, I like self-reliance. I have every confidence that I would perform very well in that position but you have to agree, if you were in my position, wouldn't that look like a bad business decision?

VP: I think you're limiting your vision, but give it some thought and get back with me.

HG: I don't want to waste any of the time you need to find someone. If those are the only terms available, I'll have to turn it down.

VP: What kind of terms would you find agreeable?

HG: In sales I create my own security based on performance tracked directly to the bottom line. That's not true in management. I've noticed a high turnover rate in management here. A lot of good sales reps are gone now who made the same move you're proposing to me. I'd want a three-year no-cut contract with a guaranteed income, not even as high as I'm making now, but it'll have to be between $100,000 to $200,000. Then I could consider doing the job with the commitment and energy I put into my work now.

VP: They'll never go for that.

Now who's not being a team player? They want you to give up more money than most people earn, but just ask them to back up their so-called promotion with a legally binding contract guaranteeing your position and income and see how quickly they crabwalk. Crabs don't scuttle as fast.

The truth is, you already have a team—the sales team. What the executives are saying to you is that they want you to leave your team and play on theirs. But they're not willing to compensate you fairly for the change. Therefore you're not what they call a team player. I call it something different:

> **suck·er** (suk' ər) n. 1. Informal. a. One who is easily deceived; a dupe.

I've personally experienced this scenario and conversation in three companies, several different times in each one. It usually happens a few months after the latest VP du jour comes on board. Unfortunately, only rarely does a company come up with appropriate compensation to retain a top manager of salespeople. When a company does, I applaud them; when they don't, it's only Standard Operating Procedure. I consider the effective sales manager the single most valuable person in a company, next to an effective CEO. But frequent scenarios like the one above produce the phony rationalization that:

"The top sales rep rarely makes a good sales manager."

Hogwash. The only reason companies endorse this propaganda is because they're not willing to pay what it costs for a sales manager who will blow the doors off and allow that position the authority to run the sales force in a truly effective manner. So what if it is McHale's Navy? So they have their own island, water ski behind the PT boat and party hard? They also save the Pacific fleet by sinking an enemy aircraft carrier in the clutch. In every sales position I've ever had, the very best sales manager (district, area, regional whatever you want to call it) was someone whose briefcase I would have gladly carried into a call. Why? Because the reason I was #1 instead of #2 in sales was due to this guy being promoted into management.

Why did he become sales manager if he was such a tremendous sales rep? Because he:

a) Created a compensation package so he could afford the job.

b) Was willing to play office politics with the H.O.E.'s (Home Office Executives).

The H.O.E.'s know they won't pay enough to get the top producing sales rep to take the job. It isn't a business thing; it's an ego thing. Their petty pride about who gets the most credit and makes the most money doesn't allow them to pay what it costs for a sales manager the other reps respect for ability and proven track record. They don't invest in someone who knows what it takes to close deals day in and day out for their company, someone who can work on joint calls, help close deals, train the sales force with result-oriented behavior and multiply their skills and experience throughout the sales force. That makes too much sense; but more to the point, they feel too threatened by a single person who can build a Super Bowl Champion in a few short years. So they fire him . . .

Then what do they do? They offer the position to mediocre also-rans who would actually get a raise in pay for taking the job. The sales production of these management selections is so mediocre that they don't make any real money. Therefore they jump at the chance for a position in management because it shows on their résumé that they're promotable. (Keep your promotion, just pay me the money.)

Unfortunately, instead of having a truly talented Ten (on a scale of zero to ten, ten being high) leading the salespeople, teaching them how to become Tens, they have a Five. A bourgeois, a mediocre achiever. A Five is someone the H.O.E.'s can control. A Five won't stand up at risk for the sales staff. A Five won't make waves. A Five hires Threes and Fours because Fives don't want to bring in anyone who can draw a gun faster than they can. They're afraid that when somebody else looks good, they look bad.

Now, what happens to a top-producing Ten selling under a Five? At best, the Five has the sense to leave the Ten alone, usually out of fear. At worst, the Five tries to clip the wings of the Ten so the Five can demonstrate that he or she is doing things with the best interest of the company in mind, thereby becoming a Company Man or Company Woman and eligible for more promotions.

The truth, obviously, is that this is just the opposite of the best interest of the company. The best interest of the company is to increase profits by increasing sales, by hiring, training, leading and supporting the best sales reps available—Tens.

Tens find the one other Ten in the group and hang out with that person. Eights and Nines look for the Tens to learn how to be like them. Sixes join large groups of Sixes for security in numbers. Sixes are just a little above average. Sixes are team players.

Professional Selling and Professional Sports

Business owners need to realize they are not unlike owners of professional sports franchises. Sales reps are their athletes. Even one top player can make a franchise successful during expansion. Even one super rep can save a fledgling operation. It's the stars who bring in the cash. People pay to see them play well and to see their team win. The same with professional sales reps. Clients pay money to the person who takes care of their needs and whose company is a winner.

The question is, why are professional sports franchise owners more aware of this than so many other owners of businesses? George Steinbrenner—Jerry Jones; New York Yankees—Dallas Cowboys; 1996 and 1998 World Series Champions—1993, '95, '96 Super Bowl Champions. Why? Because whether you like these owners or not, they know what it takes to beat the competition. They pay the price to get the top players. The 1996 World Champion New York Yankees had a total team salary of $66,000,000, the highest in Major League Baseball. Troy Aikman's contract alone is $50,000,000; Emmit Smith's is $42,000,000; Deion Sanders' is $35,000,000.

A recent *USA TODAY* article chronicled the Yankees for the 25 years since Steinbrenner took their helm. "Since then, his Yankees have won more games than any team in the major leagues, and he has issued more pink slips than Victoria's Secret."

"The American Dream Comes To Life" is a videotape program that chronicles the life of Mickey Mantle, one of the great team-players of all time. In this biography, he says, "Everybody says to me, 'How much do you think you'd make now if you were still playing?' and I like what Joe DiMaggio said. He said he would go up and knock on the door at Yankee Stadium and when George Steinbrenner opened the door, he'd say, 'Hi, partner.' I've always liked that."

BEWARE
CARDINAL RICHELIEU

*L*ike *"The Magnificent Seven"*, Alexandre Dumas' *The Three Musketeers* can easily be converted into a playful metaphor of American business. Simply re-cast the major characters:

Louis XIII, King of France	C.E.O.
Armand Duplessis, Cardinal de Richelieu	CFO, COO, GM
Anne of Austria, Queen of France	VP, Sales
M. Tréville, Captain of the Musketeers	Sales Manager
Athos, Musketeer	Sales Rep
Porthos, Musketeer	Sales Rep
Aramis, Musketeer	Sales Rep
D'Artagnan, Rookie	Sales Rep
Mme. Bonacieux	Admn. Asst.
Countess de Winter, the Cardinal's confederate	Chargebacks
Chevalier de Rochefort	Dir. / Accounting

The value in making this comparison lies in that Dumas' swashbuckling romance of the 1620's gives us an unparalleled example of a classic serpentine character—Cardinal Richelieu—the nemesis of Hired Guns everywhere.

King Louis XIII seems charmed by this reptile; after all, the Cardinal is one of the highest ranking personages in the Catholic Church. But the Cardinal fancies himself a rival to the King's power, and not long after his introduction we see that he only feigns allegiance to Louis XIII through his ecclesiastical persona while his inner darkness constantly schemes to achieve his personal agenda of power. The Cardinal knows he cannot directly challenge the King's sovereignty, so he seeks to control everything—and everyone—else under the throne. This includes the Queen, M. Tréville, and those perennial thorns in the Cardinal's side, the Musketeers, even though this executive chain of command is completely aside from Richelieu's own.

The Musketeers report exclusively to the King. They are literally his personal Hired Guns, revered for their loyalty, valiance and agile swordplay. And Dumas' description of M. Tréville's soldiers even sounds similar to the way many people view sales reps:

" . . . a legion of devil-may-care fellows, perfectly undisciplined as regarded every one but himself.

"Loose, deep drinkers, truculent, the King's Musketeers, or rather M. de Tréville's, swaggered about in the cabarets, the public walks, and at the public sports, shouting, twisting their mustaches, clanking their swords, and taking great pleasure in annoying the guards of M. le Cardinal whenever they could fall in with them."

Of M. Tréville himself, Dumas emphasizes the captain's loyalty, how he is always there for his Musketeers, whether killed—certainly to be avenged—or imprisoned, always there to claim them.

"Thus M. de Tréville was praised to the highest note by these men, who absolutely adored him, and who, ruffians though they were, trembled before him like schoolboys before their master, obedient to his least word, and ready to sacrifice themselves to wash out the smallest insult. . . The captain of the Musketeers, then, was admired, feared, and loved, a condition which constitutes the apogee of human fortunes."

Now, These Are Team Players!

What more team-oriented slogan can there possibly be than, "one for all and all for one?" What more loyal, talented and dedicated group of professionals is there than the King's Musketeers? This is the sales force that is loyal to The Boss and the company. Its sworn mission is to protect the kingdom (i.e. produce revenues to keep it strong). Sales reps report to one line of command through various sales managers and sales executives up to The Boss. The minions of the Cardinal usually follow a distinctly different line of command, whether it's accounting, operations, production, MIS, or some other non-sales function. And this is fine, as long as we maintain the separation of church and state . . .

The reason for friction between different departments is seldom due to personnel on equal levels. It almost always comes from the top. The King versus the Cardinal; CEO versus financial backers, stockholders, CFO, COO or whomever. Most intelligent sales reps know that their colleagues in other departments vitally affect their ability to sell. Sales reps have natural gregarious tendencies, they want to work well with accounting, production, operations, etc. They know who tallies their commissions, who produces the products that must satisfy client needs, who supports the smooth flow of business in the company. Trouble that gets stirred up intra-company is usually due to Cardinal Richelieu trying to control the company in a lust for power born from insecurity. ("No way should a sales rep make more money than me!") This insecurity is only agitated by the sight of self-secure, successful ("flamboyant, arrogant") sales reps.

Let me cite an example from a recent business environment in which I was employed. This company had a King and a Queen, literally a married couple who privately owned and ran the business. King Max was as brilliant a man as you would ever meet; Queen E. had the entrepreneurial gifts of building not one, but several very successful businesses. They were a joy to work with and to work for. They had a small loyal group of sales reps (three, by the way) under one sales manager, and they had Cardinal Richelieu.

In this company, sales required technical support in order to fully represent the involved workings of its high-tech products. We were fortunate to draft Adam, one of the customer service tech-support guys, into the sales division to help with in-field calls. Adam originally reported to the Cardinal, therefore this transfer required no little political maneuvering with the King and Queen.

We needed Adam's duties to be 100% pre-sales, but had to compromise his responsibilities in order to obtain his release into sales. As part of the deal, Adam was also charged with the responsibility of training clients which, though necessary, took away from his ability to be available for sales calls and other sales support functions. Due to his help with us in the field, sales grew substantially. Therefore, so did the need for training new clients, and so did the desire to have him out in the field with us.

Due to three of us booking him on numerous calls, coupled with in-house and on-site training sessions, circumstances rapidly reached the point where Adam spent only five calendar days a month at home with his children.

We put in a request to draft another person from tech-support, Hector, into a similar position in sales. The prospect of this additional help made us very optimistic about opportunities to blow the lid off previous sales records. But we kept getting mixed signals from various directions about Hector leaving customer tech-support and joining us. Hector met with us several times and said he was ready and enthused to make the move as soon as he was approved to do so. Still, weeks, then months went by; no Hector in sales. Despite continued requests, it didn't happen.

Then one day Hector turned in his resignation with three weeks notice. One of our clients hired him away for a 30% increase in income. He would have made more money than this increase once things got rolling for him in the sales department, but with nothing happening in that direction, he couldn't afford to turn down the outside offer. Before his departure, Hector met with our sales manager and said, "I wanted to come over and work with you guys. It looked like a lot of fun, but

Cardinal Richelieu told me directly that it was a big mistake letting Adam come over in the first place. He said there hasn't been any increase in sales since Adam came over, that it only hurt tech-support and he'll never allow anybody to come over to sales from tech-support again."

Our sales manager was speechless. Certainly the opposite was true; Adam was instrumental in the sale of many large and important deals. Nevertheless, the company lost Hector, and we knew we had a fight on our hands if we were to garner any additional sales support personnel.

To top it off, only a couple days later our sales manager was flabbergasted once again. He came out of his weekly Monday morning audience with the King, Queen and Cardinal Richelieu in utter disbelief after hearing the Cardinal say, "It's too bad we lost Hector. I wanted him to go over into sales. I know things have been good over there ever since Adam went and it would really help out with training and sales calls. It's really too bad we couldn't hold onto him. I really wanted to keep him." True story.

The Cardinal was commonly quoted saying things like, "I run this company," and "I'm the best salesperson here." He liked to jump in and try to claim credit in some way for every sale that was made (due to the some minimal thing like a prospect talking with our tech-support before buying, or talking with a reference the Cardinal claimed to know before they signed the deal.) Of course, if the deal turned south and did not close, he developed acute amnesia about the whole affair. We had one particular deal, as huge in revenue as it was in international name recognition, that hinged on the favorable reports of the prospective client's emissary, who we'll call Johnny Appleseed. Johnny knew those of us in sales from frequent meetings and trade shows, and had been friendly with our sales manager for years. As the deal came close to closing, the attention given to sales was too much for the Cardinal. He just had to get involved somehow, so during four-way meetings with King, Queen, Sales Manager and the Cardinal, Richelieu spouted, "Oh, I know Johnny Appleseed very well. We go way back, we go way back together," and continued to crow about how he knew that our program did everything this client needed. "Piece of cake," was, I believe, the expression he used.

Well, guess what . . . the international company bought the program with such enthusiasm they were already looking at putting it into several of their branches immediately after the first site—their corporate home office. Unfortunately, that's about when the program failed. It did not do what the client needed, and normal operations/technical support couldn't pull it out. The King and Queen called in an outside SWAT Team of technical experts from all over the nation and flew them to the client's home office to get the job done in the interest of a) taking care of the client, and b) protecting the company's reputation. The "piece of cake" ended up taking weeks of intensive effort and high costs to bake and never rose. After months of exhaustive efforts, the deal completely died.

The Plot Thins

Meanwhile, Johnny Appleseed telephoned our sales manager that he intended to personally visit our offices (for the first time) to discuss the matter with the King and Queen. When this was announced at their next meeting, the Cardinal was asked to schedule himself to be available for meetings with his Auld acquaintance. Mysteriously, he kept avoiding any commitment to be present.

"Oh, well, I don't know him that well," he said finally.

"But I thought you said you go way back with him?" asked our sales manager.

"Oh, well, that's only over the telephone. I've never actually met him," he answered.

Hey, look, I'm not making this up. I'm not that good at fiction. It seems that every company has one of these characters in it, and they are paid high salaries for their positions. If they would just stick to their own jobs and refrain from meddling in areas outside their responsibilities (like sales), we would be much more productive, if only due to reduced political distractions. But people so often want to get a hand in taking credit for a sale because the closing of a deal and the value it brings to the company carries such a high profile. How often have you heard it said, "Everybody thinks they're a salesman?" Say, Cardinal, if you really are the best sales rep here, we've got this boof open over here . . .

Identify Your Cardinal Richelieu

You probably already know who it is, but telltale signs of Cardinal Richelieu are commonly used Yes-Man phrases in the presence of the King, such as: "You're exactly right," or "I wish I'd thought of that," or "I like what you're saying," whatever may be pleasing to the King's ear. Our particular Richelieu was so good at these that we bought a Yes-Man talking doll that we kept handy for general amusement. You just snapped your fingers and it exclaimed these exact phrases and more. (Our favorite was "Whatever you're thinking, I know it must be right!") When our Queen saw it she noted of her own volition that it bore a striking resemblance to the Cardinal, then added slyly, "I hope you don't think I'm stupid."

From what I could tell, the Cardinal's own people despised him more than anyone. It stands to reason, I suppose. They were forced to deal with him daily, whereas we had the benefit of distance by officially being in a different division of the company. He threw his own first lieutenant under the bus so many times we half expected the poor guy to go postal on us one day by turning his tie into a headband and opening up with an Uzi. Even though I was in sales I often received phone calls at home from people on the Cardinal's staff trying to organize a mutiny. To some of them the issue had reached the stage of, "It's either me or him. . ."

A Word About Mutinies

I don't advocate them. Very rarely do they result in a good that is better than the bad they eliminate—and the penalty is hanging. The bottom line is, American business may be *like* war, but it isn't war. This is not a battle you can win like those in which enemies are terminated. These proceedings are civil, not criminal. You don't like the Cardinal; indeed, you may despise him or her, but your company needs the services he or she provides. Whether your personal Richelieu is your CFO, COO, GM or other management executive, the job he or she performs is important enough to the operation of your business that royalty keeps him/her around.

So What's The Bottom Line?

Deal with it. (See Chapter 24: "Do The Deal") If you invest an inordinate amount of time and energy into combating this cur you take that same time and energy away from doing what pays you—selling. So who wins? The Cardinal; nothing pleases this Eminence more than seeing sales reps flounder, regardless of the reason.

Yes, the Cardinal is a royal pain in the ass whose character resides somewhere between mischievousness and evil. But the odds on getting this miscreant terminated are very long indeed. Even if you're successful in this endeavor, one Cardinal is often replaced by another of similar ilk. So what are your options?

a) **Deal With Him/Her Directly?**—This is usually ineffective, as a show of hands tells a cheat what cards you're holding. Besides, this is not a character you are likely to change. If you find yourself suddenly attacked in either open or closed forum, however, I strongly recommend a show of force far greater than that of your attacker. Cowards always back down. But watch your back; they manage somehow to slither away, then lay plans to come back at you through more surreptitious means.

b) **Approach The Boss Directly?**—This is also usually ineffective because The Boss is the one who hires the Cardinal, therefore The Boss will naturally seek first to defend that decision.

c) **Steady As She Goes**—Keep your focus on your job at hand. The most debilitating weakness you can show is to allow this conniving knave to reduce your effectiveness, your production, your contribution, your income. (See Chapter 24.)

d) **Maintain Your Integrity**—If you connive to set the Cardinal up for disrepute, you stoop to play at that level. Instead, declare your loyalty to the King, the Queen, the company and your immediate manager. Then,

---

**Speak softly and carry a big stick;
you will go far.**
—*Theodore Roosevelt*

Another way to look at it is,

**Give 'em enough rope;
they'll hang themselves.**
—*Law of The Hired Gun*

---

*footnote: This Cardinal in this example followed the Cardinal Rule: A year after I left for greener pastures, the Queen fired him. He had jeopardized too many important sales because of his political games and ruined the positive esprit-de-corps that existed prior to his arrival.

"M"—WORLD CLASS SALES MANAGER

> ## You can't push the wheelbarrow and ride in it, too.
> —*Hired Gun Law for Managers*

ave you ever noticed how James Bond's Secret Service is set up just like any efficient sales organization? 007 is a sales number for encoding commissions. Miss Moneypenny is the sales manager's secretary. M is the sales executive over the firm's elite sales force. The PM, of course, is The Boss.

In the books by Ian Fleming, they all work for a company known as "Universal Exports." Bond even poses as an industrial chemical salesperson in *You Only Live Twice*. But whenever I draw this tongue-in-cheek comparison it's M who impresses me most, for he is truly the consummate manager of Hired Guns—no easy position, I assure you.

Whenever Bond enters M's office, the superior officer is preoccupied. Paperwork. Sometimes he hardly looks up at Bond as he scribbles one report or another. He may be a gruff old coot, but he commands Bond's respect. You can tell with one look at Bernard Lee's character that he's been where Bond is going. He knows the ropes and isn't about to mollycoddle some mediocre performer. It's excellence or out. He doesn't try to be Bond's friend; that's not why they're there.

M's is a thankless position. Wedged between an arrogant group of prima donnas and The Boss, he's the one person truly responsible for the bottom line. If Bond fouls up an assignment, it's M who answers to #10 Downing Street. But he knows Bond is the best agent in the double-O

Section and backs him to the hilt. Let's analyze a day at the double-O office and compare it with a similar scenario in the business world of a large advertising agency:

Thunderball: M has sent Bond to Shrublands, a naturalist spa, for a mandatory two-week rest and recovery due to the extreme nature of his lifestyle. Nearing the end of his stay, Bond receives an urgent communiqué and speeds toward the home office in London. He arrives in the office after narrowly escaping a high speed car chase that ends with his enemy exploding from an unidentified motorcycle's rocket-guided sidecar. Following is a dilemma in 007's world compared with a parallel scenario showing Bond as an ad agency account supervisor:

Moneypenny:
"You're late!"

Bond:
"Yes, some people on
the roads really burn you
up these days."
(He heads toward M's office.)

Moneypenny:
"Uh-unh. In the
conference room.
Something pretty big.
Every double-0 man
in Europe has been
rushed in. And the
Home Secretary, too."

Bond:
"Somebody probably
lost a dog . . ."

Moneypenney:
"You're late!"

Bond:
"Yes, how empty my life
would be without pagers
and voice-mail."
(He heads toward M's office)

Moneypenny:
"Uh-unh. In the
conference room.
Something pretty big.
Every major account rep
in the nation has been
rushed in. And the
home office VP, too."

Bond:
"Somebody probably
lost a bet . . ."

Bond strides across a marble conference room floor; his is the only chair still empty. Just before he sits, M stands and remarks,

M:
"Well, now that we're all here . . ."

A British bomber carrying two nuclear warheads has disappeared, and the government has received an audio tape ransoming Great Britain for $100,000,000 by S.P.E.C.T.R.E. M has his business plan well organized. First, he has all known information of the plan neatly packaged. Each agent is given a complete dossier with all information pertinent to the matter. At the appropriate time, M instructs the agents

Bond slips through wood veneer conference room doors and slips across wall-to-wall carpet to take the only empty chair. Just before he sits, M stands and remarks,

M:
"Well, now that we're all here . . ."

The agency has just received notice that its biggest client, Budweiser, is moving its $100,000,000 account to a rival agency. The home office has called all major account execs from across the country into a meeting at Bond's branch office. M has his business plan well organized. First, he has all information relevant to the firm's plan neatly packaged. Each account supervisor is given a complete facts file with all information relevant to their assignment enclosed. At the appropriate time, M instructs the account execs

when the files may be
opened. He then has
individual meetings
with each agent in
his office to discuss
their assignments.

M:
"I've assigned
you to Station C,
Canada."

Bond:
"Sir, I respectfully
suggest that you
change my assignment
to Nassau."

M:
"Is there any other
reason, besides your
enthusiasm for water sports?"

Bond:
"Perhaps this, sir."
(He hands M a photo.)

M:
"Well?"

Bond:
"Well, there was
a photograph of that

when the files may be
opened. He then has
individual meetings
with each exec in
his office to discuss
their assignments.

M:
"I've assigned
you to go after
Coors."

Bond:
"Sir, I respectfully
suggest that you
change my assignment
to RJ Reynolds."

M:
"Is there any other reason,
besides your
appreciation of cigarettes?"

Bond:
"Perhaps this, sir."
(He hands M a memo and a photo)

M:
"Well?"

Bond:
"Well, that's an internal
memo I obtained during

man in this dossier you gave us. His name is Derval. I saw him last night at Shrublands. But he was dead."

Capt. Pritchett:
"Oh no, sir. Not possible. He was seen boarding the Vulcan; took off last night."

M:
"If 007 says he saw Derval last night at Shrublands and he was dead, then that's enough for me to initiate inquiries."

Capt. Pritchett:
"Oh well, yes sir. Of course."

M: (studying the photo)
"Who is this girl?"

Bond:
"Derval's sister, sir."

a lunch date yesterday. It suggests RJR is considering agency reviews. A friend of mine is in charge of their media buying."

Mr. Pritchett:
"Oh no, sir. Not possible. They've had the same agency for decades. Practically married to them, I'd say."

M:
"If Bond says the Reynolds account may come up for reviews and has a source, then that's enough for me to initiate inquiries."

Mr. Pritchett:
"Oh well, yes sir. Of course."

M: (studying the photo)
"Who is this girl?"

Bond:
"My friend, sir."

M:
"Do you know
where she is now?"

M:
"Do you know how
strong her position is?"

Bond:
"Nassau."

Bond:
"VP of Media."

M:
"Hmm—Do you
think she's worth
going after?"

M:
"Hmm—Do you
think she's worth
going after?"

Bond:
"I wouldn't have
put it quite that
way, sir."

Bond:
"I wouldn't have
put it quite that
way, sir."

M: (gruffly)
"You've only got
four days, 007.
Don't spend your
time sitting around."

M: (gruffly)
"You don't have
forever, Bond.
Don't spend your
time sitting around."

M tolerates 007's subtle witticisms, because:

When you own the opera house, you put up with the primma donnas.

—Law of The Hired Gun

The Boss doesn't have to put up with the dress extras or stage hands or other actors. But there's one person who draws the crowd that fills the seats and pays the tab. That prima donna gets treated differently than everyone else.

The same is true in any business, as is evidenced outside M's office at Moneypenny's desk. The following scene fits both our parallel scenarios. Watch as the executive secretary studies the photo and Bond looks on:

Moneypenny: "Smashing figure. I don't suppose that has anything to do with your request."

Bond: "Has there ever been a man so misunderstood?"

Moneypenny: "Now James, you can't pull the wool over my eyes. You might be able to con The Old Man, but I know better . . ."

M: (enters unannounced) "So do I, Miss Moneypenny. And I'll thank you—not to refer to me as 'The Old Man.'"

Whether he's the head of Britain's Secret Service or Executive Vice-President of a huge advertising agency, M's posture is wedged between a proud group of prima donnas and The Boss. Just as the focal point of an hourglass controls sands of time, his spot governs bottom line contribution from top to bottom, and vice versa. If an agent blows an assignment or an account supervisor loses a major account it's M who answers to The Boss, whether that's #10 Downing Street or the agency's president and stockholders. Bond is his best operator, his Hired Gun— and his best chance to pull out a clutch victory; M backs him to the hilt. A Moneypenney or a Q is valuable—but not invaluable, and they don't enjoy the Hired Gun's freedoms. By contrast, Bond is insurance for everyone's paycheck. M puts up with the prima donnas, but not the stage hands.

WHEN YOU OWN THE OPERA HOUSE, YOU PUT UP WITH THE PRIMA DONNAS

*M*ost smart people who work with high achievers are savvy enough to put up with prima donnas because they appreciate their value to the company. They may think sales reps are a bunch of hot dogs, but they know it goes with the territory, just as they know that lions roar and gorillas beat their chests. It's the nature of the beast.

There is one person The Boss always makes time to see: the top producing sales rep. Consider the probability that The Boss probably has a sales background, too. About 60% of U.S. CEO's have their backgrounds in sales. Not only does The Boss know the value of input from his troops in the field, some modicum of social enjoyment is there—if only to relive bygone days of sales achievement.

Sales oriented people have high needs for verbal expression. This is what we do: talk, listen, persuade. You probably resent chickenhearted e-mail dictums; so does The Boss. A CEO wants to deal with an important person or issue face to face, not through some pale inner-office memo or ethereal e-mail.

The boss has a high need for power

Business people are driven by three basic needs: power, achievement and affiliation. Leaders normally seek power; athletes and sales reps feed on high achievement; (How do you identify a high achiever? Look around them. See many trophies, plaques, congratulatory letters, photos with important personages?) Managers, customer service and other support staff have high needs for affiliation. That's what they do, affiliate with other managers, other staff, customers, etc.

In a constructive working environment, the Hired Gun knows to submit to The Boss' need for power; The Boss knows to respect the Hired Gun's high need for verbal expression. The Boss knows that meetings are held for the benefit of the person calling the meeting. So you will be listened to. But you must remember The Boss' need for power. You'll probably have five minutes. Make it short, sweet, to the point.

The rules of this exclusive communication are:

Don't send a memo to The Boss about an important issue. Bosses tend to see memos and e-mails as coming from someone who is afraid to deal with them face to face. It's a typical move made by managers whose low self esteem can't conceive of walking in to see The Boss and talking about something important. A Boss respects someone who deals with him/her verbally and directly. It's good to detail your points in writing and leave them behind *after* your meeting for detailed reference later, but Bosses respect someone who communicates with them the way they communicate with others—face to face.

As a sales rep you talk with decision-makers daily. Your clients are probably in charge of larger operations than your own company. Your client's Boss is probably bigger than your company's Boss. So go sell The Boss like you would your client.

The Boss won't waste time listening to rambling stories. His/her high-speed mind immediately seeks the bottom line. Give it first, followed by a suggestion; then if details are requested give them. You're cut from similar cloths; neither of you wants to endure an involved story that eventually leads up to something unless it's a joke. Save jokes for more appropriate occasions.

The Boss isn't there to make friends; neither are you. Respect is the strongest bond you can establish. Earn the Boss' respect, don't try to win his/her friendship. Unless yours is a very small company you're probably not going to be invited to The Boss' house for dinner, or other per-sonal/social activities.

At one company in my experience The Boss made a dedicated effort to communicate directly with the top producers. Once a month he took the top producers of each division to a group lunch. Just The Boss and the #1 sales reps from each division. No managers. This gave an open forum of communication. And when you saw his little notebook flip out to receive the entry of a quick note, you knew action was less than an hour away.

"YOU SUCK!"
(HOW TO KNOW YOU HAVE A LOUSY SALES MANAGER)

In contrast to the preceding chapters about the working relationships between excellent sales managers and top producing sales reps, this chapter illustrates the disastrous effects that bad, really bad, sales management can have on a sales force. It leads with the true story of . . .

As you may recall from chapter five, a tactic that aroused the spirits of my high performance sales staff was showing them short, high-impact film clips just prior to getting started in the morning. Although that particularly successful example involved daily showings, that was only done for one particular week at the end of one month. We only did this when a particular timing point was right, or a particular scene had timely relevance to something happening within our ranks.

On one notable occasion, we were behind pace in our production. I had every confidence that these committed salespeople would pull out a respectable month, but wanted to motivate their pace. I brought in a video that had particular appeal to me for many reasons, and hoped it would succeed in spurring them on.

The tape was one in a series of programs by Bud Greenspan entitled, *Numero Uno*. In each show of this series he examined the life of an athlete who dominated his or her sport, without peer. The tape I showed highlighted the career of perhaps the greatest middle distance runner in history, Peter Snell of New Zealand. I chose it for this purpose because I grew up watching the trademark come-from-behind finishes of this fantastic Olympic Champion and world record holder since childhood.

Peter won three Olympic gold medals in the 800 and 1500 meters in the 1960 and 1964 games of Rome and Tokyo, respectfully. He trained for the marathon under grueling conditions so that a mere metric mile was nothing by comparison. This incredible stamina, combined with outstanding natural speed enabled him to literally run away from all competitors for many years. The most dramatic thing to see, however, was his ability to come from as far back as eighth place going into the bell lap of the 1500 meters and finish with an incredible burst that often left second place as far as thirty yards behind—against the best runners in the world.

At the time that I showed the tape our team had been programmed to respond positively to brief heroic stimuli from movies on tape. I hoped to make even greater impact with a true-life hero. I was fortunate and I was right; the effect was tremendous. You could feel the collective raising of goosepimples on every person in the room. Their eyes were wide with enthusiasm. I overheard several guys voice controlled zeal: "Wow!" "Man!" "That was incredible!" "What a kick!" "Did you see the power in his legs?" "He tore chunks of cinders up out of the track!" "They flew up in the face of the guys he passed!"

At the tape's conclusion I compared Peter's winning spirit to that of the sales team. I likened his tremendous finishing kick to the kind of all-out blast we needed to pull the month out. I challenged them to rise to their championship potential. You could see the enthusiasm in their eyes; they were really revved up—ready to charge to their desks and hit the telephones.

Shot Down In Flames

I haven't mentioned that at this particular meeting we were graced by an impromptu visit from my boss, the Wolfman. He watched the entire meeting, then took it upon himself to speak after me. He began by saying that the idea of watching the films was nice, but seeing other people do great things didn't amount to results on the sales charts. As a matter of fact, he was strongly disappointed in the current standings of the sales charts. As a matter of fact, "You Suck!"

And it went downhill from there. The man's human persona quickly faded as the Wolfman took over and chewed on some individual reps, then the group as a whole. All the positive progress we made in the meeting and the desire to excel was stomped and trodden by this immature behavior. Instead of charging down the hall to our offices, full of electricity and spirit as they had been, they shuffled like berated children.

The day was shot to hell, but we managed to pull out a successful month despite the Wolfman's ranting. How? The operative word here is "despite." He gave us a common enemy. We rallied together out of spite for his ridiculous demeaning attitude just to show what we were made of. The interesting thing is, he actually believed he was helping out by lambasting the group.

We did all right, but what little respect the sales team had for the Wolfman was lost forever. For years afterward even people who weren't there, even people who never met the Wolfman, referred to verbal lashings of a similar tone from executives as "You Suck" speeches.

YOU KNOW YOU HAVE A "YOU SUCK" MANAGER IF:

(Unfortunate references from personal experience)

♦ Sales reps are coerced to write up deals that are not yet confirmed so the manager's numbers can be achieved.

♦ Sales reps are chastised in front of their peers in order to make an example.

♦ The manager tells sales reps to kickback money from spiff awards.

♦ The manager puts a mole in your group.

♦ The manager gets upset when sales reps earn more money than he or she does. (I offered a standing $100 bonus each month to anyone who made more than I did. It was a neat thing to give out in front of the group.)

♦ Doesn't hire women or minorities because they don't fit the manager's idea of the sales program's needs. (Sure, there are laws against this, and for good reason. Now, prove it.)

- Loses temper in sales meetings. (We once had a manager literally throw a desk at a rep.)
- Embezzles from the spiff fund, doesn't award the spiff money to the reps, but pockets it.

And then there are the new VP's:

Upon arrival, immediately fires the #1 sales manager to set an example and simultaneously eliminate any power threat. (Isn't this what tough convicts do when thrown in prison?)

Installs puppet managers over each division.

Demands that every item of historical relevance be picked up by these puppets for "executive review." (No less than twenty-five boxes of papers, videotapes, sales pieces, marketing letters, etc. from our one division alone.)

Halts the progress of all pending contracts until each one is personally reviewed for the manager's blessing. (Thirteen divisions, ten reps per division, average of ten closings per rep per month, after roughly thirty proposals per rep . . . nearly 4,000 proposals held up from one month alone—significantly impedes progress on all deals.)

Stands on top of desks to speak down to the sales team.

Unbelievable Utterances:

- "When you see the new commission plan you're gonna pee your leg!"
- "Nothing personal, you just can't work here anymore."
- "You can't hurt me! I spent twenty days in a cage in Viet Nam!"
- "We're fixin' all the problems caused by that last bunch of weak-suck managers . . ."
- "Salespeople have to be treated like children."
- "Wait'll they get a load of Me!"

♦ "You may hate me during the month, but you'll love me the day you get your paycheck."
♦ "I don't give a @#%* about your wife."
♦ "I wish he'd get off the phone so I can fire him."
♦ "I don't like him. I think I'll fire him. I just don't like him."

How did we save our sanity through this parade of short-term sales managers and executives? Cartoons, practical jokes, impersonation contests. The management/leadership adage is true that the character of a company is carried from the top down. In these cases, immaturity begot immaturity. If you find yourself in this kind of setting, go get a real job. It may not be as much fun, but you'll respect yourself in the morning.

NOTHING HAPPENS UNTIL SOMETHING IS SOLD

A *hackneyed phrase, to be sure,* but too often forgotten as the bottom line #1 canon of commerce:

> ## Nothing happens until something is sold.
> —*Law of The Hired Gun*

Any Junior Achievement student knows that businesses exist to provide services and make profits. But businesses don't make money on what they produce; they make money on what they sell. In order to create sales, businesses must employ people who can sell. Therefore, sales reps are vital to the success of businesses.

The reason for this rather elementary syllogistic argument is that too often those not in sales attempt to belittle the value of the group that brings in the revenue for everybody's paychecks, the sales reps. The classic rebuttal is that without the widgets produced by the company, there would be nothing to sell.

Let me tell you something, Harvey; if you don't have a product that's ready to sell, you're not in business anyway. The bottom line of any business is revenue and profits, not the inventory of widgets. Production can yield mountains of widgets, but without sales the mountains eventually rot and rust away and the production department doesn't draw a paycheck. Then what do all those non-sales departments do? They go somewhere that has an effective sales effort to produce widgets where they'll be paid for their efforts. The end result is money and there's only one department that produces this valuable commodity—sales.

Everybody in the company is in sales.

Another commonly espoused business adage, but do the personnel in your organization practice this? Each and every prospect and client needs to be treated by everyone in the company as if that one prospect or that one paying client is vital to the survival of the company, because they are.

Whatever happened to "The customer is always right?"

Companies could make internal and external communications much simpler if they merely re-titled the two people sitting on the right and left hand of The Boss:

PRO-ACTIVE VP
A N D
RE-ACTIVE VP

Sales is active; it's hunter-gatherer. It goes out and makes things happen. Everything else in a company is reactive to what sales causes to happen.

    a. Accounting counts the money sales brings in, then allocates it for the company's needs.

    b. Production makes the products/services to fill the orders sales creates.

    c. Customer Service interacts with customers who have bought because of sales.

    d. HR/Personnel hires employees paid by the revenues generated from sales.

    e. Management—manages, usually to alienate sales in some way.

Some business authorities may think this argument smacks of Sales Chauvinism; they're right. I invite them to consider the consequences of replacing their top sales reps with order takers. Sometimes this is actually considered because order-takers cost less and are easy to manage.

And order-taking is a nice job. You sit at a desk, answer the phone, write up what somebody decides they want from a catalog, punch the time-clock for an hourly wage, go home. No conflict, no stress. Order takers are a viable business entity. They handle the routine deals that would not engage the talents of strong sales hunter-gatherers and if teamed together can be very effective.

But imagine James Bond writing parking tickets

When the high achievers are gone, and there are only those with low comfort levels left, I suggest these same authorities analyze what happens to the growth, revenue and stock prices of the company.

I was at one company where the COO (a textbook CPA) was overheard from a closed door meeting and forever quoted referring to sales as "that bunch of marketing scum."

And we wonder why it's vital to forge a secure self-image . . .

You will inevitably deal with someone who is not OK with your success in sales. They will try to make you feel un-OK with yourself and your job in an attempt to pull you down to their level so they can feel a little better about their chosen station. Here are some suggested rebuttal tactics:

1) Salespeople have the opportunity to make a lot of money; they also have the opportunity to make no money.

2) For those who think the job is easy, there is always a boof or territory open. Invite them to try their hand at the job and the unpredictable income opportunity.

3) Of any profession, sales has the highest Return On Investment.

Doctors, lawyers, architects, engineers, etc. all go to school for years, earn several degrees, then go out and set up practices with expensive overheads of offices, staffs, equipment, books, journals, etc. Salespeople can start right out of school, make unlimited incomes, and not have the huge overheads associated with law libraries and staffs, medical or dental equipment and staffs, etc.

4) Compensation—The entire sales compensation plan should require no more than one paragraph of twenty-five words or less. The more complicated the sales compensation plan, the more it is designed to screw with commissions. If they want to make it open and honest, it states a flat amount of base, draw, etc. and a clearly drawn percentage of sales revenues as commission. Bonuses and spiffs are also clear and direct. When you get plans that involve "ifs" and "thens" and conditions based on the Theory of Magnetic Resonance and the Laws of Give and Take, you might as well get ready for a prostate exam.

DO THE DEAL

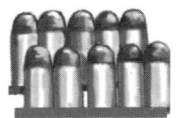

*T*op *sales reps are compensated* for one job and one job only, closing deals. To do this successfully demands an intense focus on finding prospects, getting in front of them, making presentations, answering objections and questions, analyzing financial scenarios, helping them figure out how to go ahead and buy, then getting the actual paperwork signed and turned in. For many sales reps this must be accomplished with a number of different clients each month in order to make a living. Ironically, executives and management often concoct corporate strategies that distract salespeople from the vital intensity needed to do their jobs.

When I worked at the telemarketing company it was just this way. We needed to close anywhere from eight to twenty deals a month to make real money. All this was done over the telephone: building a pipeline, keeping on top of every prospect, herding them all along toward consummation, getting those agreements signed and faxed in. These were sales of revenue between $10,000 to $30,000 each. Sometimes we'd begin and close a deal within two weeks, sometimes it would take two years or more. Our focus was naturally intense, but we still had to wear blinders to keep from being distracted by the trivialities that management cooked up to justify its existence.

Every new division in the company started like it was shot from a cannon; the newest project always got the most attention. Collateral materials were produced that represented our value to prospects. Sales materials were abundant; spiffs were strong. And though new salespeople started out with no more training than having computers and telephones on their desks, our division signed up new subscribers at the rate of over sixty per month with revenues approaching $500,000 monthly. Sales and morale were high, spiff money flowed.

The Honeymoon Is Over

Eventually reality crept in and the problems of day to day operations made themselves evident, as in any business. Monthly program schedules were delivered late, after the month began; clients didn't receive the products they ordered; clients who were acquired by any of the numerous mergers and acquisitions flying around the industry canceled due to new management or new budgets.

But at one point the decision was made to hold sales accountable for any cancellations of service that occurred. It was mandated that commissions that were earned from a particular deal would be subtracted from a commission check if that client canceled for any reason whatsoever.

What did sales have to do with cancellations? The reasons clients canceled were that they had cutbacks in budget, or they never received their products from the fulfillment department, or received no technical support, or our accounting department fouled up their invoicing, or misappropriated checks—then threatened to cut them off for non-payment. The only responsibility of salespeople was to close deals and get the agreements signed. Sales was not responsible for customer service; we had a customer service department for that. Irrelevant; sales was the only department that was to be held financially accountable if clients canceled.

Meetings increased in frequency while we argued these points. Meanwhile, management decided that lagging sales were due to inadequate activity: not enough telephone calls every day, not enough phone time per call, not enough sales collaterals sent out daily. During myriad meetings in which we argued these points we lost the very hours and days of active selling time they were complaining about. Then we ran out of sales materials and it took weeks to get them delivered to us. Meanwhile, if we didn't sell we didn't get paid. It was like being at war and running out of ammunition and gasoline. Yet we still managed to make sales. Sneezy said, "They give us sticks and stones and we build Cadillacs."

They were right about one thing, though. Sales numbers were taking it on the chin. Somehow they failed to consider that it was due to significant drops in morale and low levels of desire to do the job. Under this ridiculous system of chargebacks due to cancellations, a sales rep who sold $50,000 revenue in a month had $30,000 taken away because of clients that canceled. This deduction of commissionable revenue was taken before commissions were calculated, and resulted in commissions paid on a net of $20,000 revenue instead of the $50,000 produced. Sales reps were personally financially penalized for factors completely out of the control of the sales reps.

Sales' response? Find out early if clients were going to cancel. If they were, those sales reps didn't log any sales during that month. They'd turn them all in to log huge production the following month, when they didn't have any cancellations. Management's reaction to this plan was that anyone caught holding deals and cashing them in en masse would be fired. Executive management made a game-playing policy, sales reps responded with a plan to play the game to win, but if they executed the plan they would be fired.

Meanwhile, other non-closing job duties were handed to sales reps to handle, such as customer service calls from all the clients in a rep's territory. I have nothing against customer service; in fact, I'm very big on it. But in most cases it should be handled by the customer service department, not the sales reps. Yet here we were taking twenty calls a day from clients. We couldn't concentrate on selling. If the customer service department couldn't do the job they needed to fix that department, not foist that job off on sales.

It was in the heat of this fray that I sat down and penned a message to myself with a broad green felt-tipped marker:

Avoid Distractions

Do the Deal!

Renewals are NOT the deal.

Customer Service is NOT the deal.

Collections is NOT the deal.

Meetings are NOT the deal.

In the end, nobody cares about how many renewals you did, now much your clients like you, how much money you collected, what meetings you did. You are recognized and paid for one thing:

DO THE DEAL

I posted this on a single sheet of paper in my boof, right over the telephone. It was interesting that many managers came by my boof, obviously saw the bold declaration, but never commented on it. A week later I noticed a photocopy of my piece in another guy's boof. A few weeks later it popped up in several more. Eventually it spread throughout the company in all other divisions. Then it was creatively typeset on a computer and multiplied. It was simply a personal reminder to maintain focus on the job at hand, but apparently it struck a cord.

There will be times when you find yourself not producing the kinds of numbers you are known for, or expect of yourself. First, look at yourself to see if there are personal issues that distract you from your job. Then look around you at work. Are there issues there that affect your attitude, your intensity, your focus? You may want to create a personal bulletin tailored to your particular needs and post it. You might just find it multiplied among your fellows.

CONTRACT KILLER

The one who needs the deal the least, always wins.

—*Law of The Hired Gun*

You're a killer sales rep and everybody knows it. You get called several times a month by people feeling you out on your current job satisfaction. It seems there's always an opportunity to help build somebody else's business. When you become available as a free agent you get every kind of offer from promotional paddleballs and wireless cable TV to medical supplies and insurance. You're the kind of franchise player for whom sharp and needy CEOs are desperate, like in Tom Peters' case study in Chapter 3.

So why sell yourself short? If you learn nothing else from all this, please make this concept part of your Standard Operating Procedure. You know a deal isn't closed until the agreement is signed. And if you sell advertising, you never go for a one-time deal; you sell contracts because you know there's income for a term of 3x, 6x, 12x or more. If this is true for what you sell, why sell the person doing the selling for anything less?

Because of the sales profession's volatility it is vital that you establish exit plans before you go in the front door. CEO's have them, professional athletes have them, managers and coaches of college and pro teams have them, and so do marriages:

Professional Pre-Nuptials

This doesn't work for unexceptional talent, but we're not dealing with mediocrity here; we're talking about you. You're the one volunteering W-2s and year-end pay check stubs as evidence that you're the MVP this expansion team needs. If they want you to play, they have to pay.

The situation is simple supply and demand. You have rare skills; they have a high need. You're willing to risk your energy and life-force in this endeavor; what are they willing to offer as compensation?

What are you worth?

You're coming into an operation owned by someone else. Who stands to gain from the tremendous volume of revenue you will create with skills and charisma you created through years of hard knocks? They do. Exceptional sales reps often stride into a fledgling or floundering company, hit huge home runs and save the day. Unfortunately, when they leave or get fired the company retains the revenues of clients that would never have been delivered unless the Hired Gun was on staff. Make your agreements about commissions and pay plans, then paint your picture with a door behind you instead of a corner.

Get It In Writing

If they balk at the pay plan, it's not a deal but a scam. Also pay a lot of attention to the pay-out plan. This is different than the amount of your compensation. This is how you will receive the compensation due to you. It's great if a single sale will pay you $10,000, but it may not be as grand if it's paid three months after the sale is consummated, or paid out over six months' time. If they complain about a front-end contract as a term of employment, you're being set up from the outset. If the pay plan or the pay-out plan are impasses, w-a-l-k.

Remember that friend I visited for lunch—the one who lost the major client the day I swung by? The reason that turned out to be a positive business relationship between friends was because of front-end contracting. If you recall, we were somewhere in the Caribbean when she said, "I'll pay you $10,000 if you get them back." I considered the sum about three seconds and said, "OK."

Well, I left something out back there. Suddenly it changed to "Well, how about five thousand and a pentium laptop?" We were old friends and she was joking, but she was pointing out the need to come to an agreement and put it in writing. We worked out a lump sum bonus upon re-establishment of the client, commissions paid on sales of new independent retailers, a continuing percentage of the revenue from the new clients I brought in and a couple of dangling-carrot perqs that make such projects fun. It's the kind of thing you must have before you start day number one.

Take care of yourself; don't sell yourself cheaply. Take a long look into every opportunity, evaluate your odds of success, test your belief factor in the business and the people. If it all looks promising, go for it. But determine your worth to that endeavor and create an agreement that puts both you and the company on the winners stand. I suggest the Aristotelian process of a beginning, a middle and an end:

The Beginning: Write a front-end contract with a no-cut clause. This establishes your responsibilities and authority from the outset, as well as your complete compensation plan. The fact that it is a "No-Cut" arrangement means that regardless of the reason for termination you get paid. Professional coaches, athletes and business executives have this, why not sales reps?

The Middle: Compensation should be spelled out directly and succinctly. Signing bonus, production bonus, commissions on sales, any draw or base, expenses, car allowances, etc. They might argue that they don't do this with the other sales employees. Fine; those are the same people whose lack of production got them in the jam they're in now.

The End: It will come; it always does whether in one year or ten, but we've covered that point. Make sure that when it does you are financially prepared. Build in a severance package or a bonus for long term results that you will produce. As much as I hate to say it, you may need to get an attorney involved.

THERE'S ALWAYS SOMEBODY FASTER

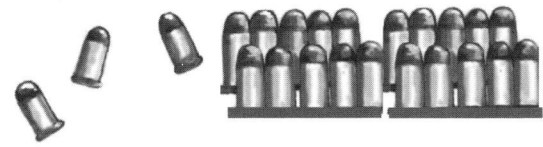

> ## Speed costs money. How fast do you want to go?
> *—Law of The Hired Gun*

I hated having to sell my first Ferrari. Consequently, it wasn't long before I wanted a high performance car again in the worst way. (It was spring!) A guy at work had connections in the car business and showed up one day with a dark green ZR-1 Corvette. I was never partial to plastic cars, but this one had performance out the wazoo and a price tag I could afford. I eagerly awaited lunchtime to drive it through its paces.

We hit 90 mph in the company parking lot and stopped on a dime. The car did everything: slammed you back in the seat, turned tightly, handled well, stopped on command. Everything a car should do. I named it Godzilla. The guy did me a disservice when he said he could procure one of these monsters for a very reasonable price; much less than I'd pay for another Ferrari. I lost a good deal of selling time that afternoon daydreaming about it.

That evening I felt like Snoopy in a vicarious experience as the World War I Flying Ace as I waited to zoom onto the highway in my trusty pickup truck. I imagined myself taxiing the on-ramp in the green monster, ready to pounce the unsuspecting herd of cars as they trotted home. I visualized blasting through gaps in traffic and hitting 150 before the weight of numbers forced me to cool the jets.

Suddenly a flash of red roared past and disappeared—a Ferrari F-40. In an instant my dreams of invincibility were crushed. The ZR-1 is an awesome performance machine capable of 179 mph, but the F-40 tops

200, and in less time. I would have pulled out on my very first day and been run down by a prancing horse before I'd driven a furlong. And as anyone who has ever hot rodded knows, when you square off on the highway, speed is all that matters; price is not the point.

My dad had a way of keeping my head within its hat size when I was young and winning a lot of medals in track and field. First I won county championships, then a state record, then the fastest time in the nation in my event. Nevertheless, he subtly reminded me that around any corner there could be an All-American or World Champion or Olympic Gold Medalist.

You may be the fastest gun in your group, maybe in the entire sales force of a nationwide company. And that's GREAT! But what about those reps who sell private jets, or corporate takeovers or billion-dollar telephone switches? No matter who you are, you never have the fastest car, or gun.

It doesn't hurt to take a few moments once a week and remember who gave you the talent, the charisma, the opportunities and the rewards . . . and say thanks. A healthy self-image is the best thing we can have, but we only have it because the Lord above gives it to us. Besides, we both know that the best you and I can do is to fool some of the people, all of the time.

REWRITE YOUR IDENTITY

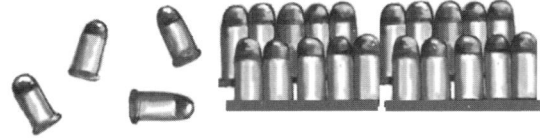

*R*emember, *"Writing is rewriting* what you've already rewritten." DO THIS EXERCISE. This revision is the one that gets you there. If it was easy, anybody could do it. This isn't for just anybody. It's for you. Go for it!

_____

_____

_____

_____

_____

_____

_____

_____

_____

_____

_____

_____

_____

_____

_____

_____

_____

_____

_____

_____

_____

_____

ABSOLUTELY, POSITIVELY REQUIRED READING

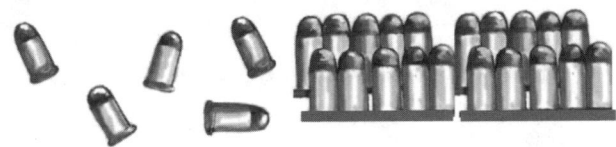

TWENTY-TWO BOOKS THAT WILL CHANGE YOUR LIFE:

1) *Think and Grow Rich*—Napoleon Hill
2) *Animal Farm*—George Orwell
3) *The Prince*—Machiavelli
4) *Plunkitt of Tammany Hall*—William Riordon
5) *Who Needs God*—H. Kushner
6) *When Bad Things Happen to Good People*—H. Kushner
7) *Lead The Field*—Earl Nightingale
8) *The Seven Habits of Highly Successful People*—Stephen R. Covey
9) *How To Win Friends and Influence People*—Dale Carnegie
10) *Be My Guest*—Conrad Hilton
11) *I, The Jury*—Mickey Spillane
12) *The Greatest Salesman In The World*—Og Mandino
13) *The Greatest Secret In The World*—Og Mandino
14) *Awaken The Giant Within*—Anthony Robbins
15) *The Tao of Pooh*—Benjamin Hoff
16) *The Book of Five Rings*—Miyamoto Musashi
17) *The Art Of War*—Sun Tzu
18) *The One Minute $alesperson*—Spencer Johnson, MD, Larry Wilson
19) *You ^{2}*—Price Pritchett
20) *Psycho-Cybernetics*—Maxwell Maltz, MD, F.I.C.S.
21) *The Magic Of Thinking Big*—David Schwartz, Ph.D.
22) *On Liberty*—John Stuart Mill

ABOUT THE AUTHOR

"Once, I closed an important advertising sale by giving my client a Tommy Gun as a clincher; the best part was getting it covered on my expense account. Another time, I met with Southland Corporation's marketing executives and handed them a baseball bat to smash my hands after my company failed to perform to the standards I promised. (Fortunately, they declined.) Later, at 7-Eleven's Christmas party these same execs handed me a check for $305,000 across the bar as a cash advance for another ad campaign. By age 30 I had over $1,000,000 in personal assets. At 35, my phone was cut off because I couldn't pay Ma Bell fifty bucks. Now I drive my second Ferrari, own a downtown warehouse where I live with my pet mountain lion. I get about a call a week from a company that needs a Hired Gun."

Robert Workman is a fighter and a gentleman, at once tough and compassionate, but mostly passionate. A popular public speaker, he has also written numerous sales training/human development programs. This twenty-year veteran salesman's consistent track record as #1 in sales includes several years among 800 advertising reps nationwide and four years in a row among 300 aggressive telemarketers. Entrepreneur, connoisseur, raconteur, his lifestyle includes Italian cars, wines and operas, Cuban cigars and James, his second South American cougar (who replaced Kuma).

STAY TUNED! COMING SOON:

TRAIL BOSS
HOW TO LEAD YOUR HIRED GUNS

To Kuma the Puma;
Top Carnivore